D0205505

DATE DUE

**A FINE WILL BE CHARGED FOR EACH
OVERDUE MATERIAL.**

EDITH WHARTON

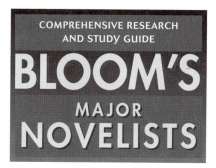

COMPREHENSIVE RESEARCH
AND STUDY GUIDE

BLOOM'S

MAJOR
NOVELISTS

EDITED AND WITH AN
INTRODUCTION BY HAROLD BLOOM

EDITH
WHARTON

COMPREHENSIVE RESEARCH
AND STUDY GUIDE

BLOOM'S
MAJOR
NOVELISTS

EDITED AND WITH AN INTRODUCTION
BY HAROLD BLOOM

© 2002 by Chelsea House Publishers, a subsidiary of
Haights Cross Communications.

Introduction © 2002 by Harold Bloom.

Printed and bound in the United States of America.

First Printing
1 3 5 7 9 8 6 4 2

Library of Congress Cataloging-in-Publication Data
Edith Wharton / edited and with an introduction by Harold Bloom.
        p. cm. — (Bloom's major novelists)
    Includes bibliographical references and index.
    ISBN 0-7910-6349-6 (alk. paper)
    1. Wharton, Edith, 1862-1937—Criticism and interpretation.
    2. Women and literature—United States—History—20th century.
    I. Bloom, Harold.   II. Series.

    PS3545.H16 Z645 2001
    813'.52—dc21   2001047497

Chelsea House Publishers
1974 Sproul Road, Suite 400
Broomall, PA 19008-0914

The Chelsea House World Wide Web address is
http://www.chelseahouse.com

Series Editor: Matt Uhler

Contributing Editor: Aislinn Goodman

Produced by Publisher's Services, Santa Barbara, California

Contents

User's Guide

This volume is designed to present biographical, critical, and bibliographical information on the author's best-known or most important works. Following Harold Bloom's editor's note and introduction is a detailed biography of the author, discussing major life events and important literary accomplishments. A plot summary of each novel follows, tracing significant themes, patterns, and motifs in the work.

A selection of critical extracts, derived from previously published material from leading critics, analyzes aspects of each work. The extracts consist of statements from the author, if available, early reviews of the work, and later evaluations up to the present. A bibliography of the author's writings (including a complete list of all works written, cowritten, edited, and translated), a list of additional books and articles on the author and his or her work, and an index of themes and ideas in the author's writings conclude the volume.

~

Harold Bloom is Sterling Professor of the Humanities at Yale University and Henry W. and Albert A. Berg Professor of English at the New York University Graduate School. He is the author of over 20 books, including *Shelley's Mythmaking* (1959), *The Visionary Company* (1961), *Blake's Apocalypse* (1963), *Yeats* (1970), *A Map of Misreading* (1975), *Kabbalah and Criticism* (1975), *Agon: Toward a Theory of Revisionism* (1982), *The American Religion* (1992), *The Western Canon* (1994), and *Omens of Millennium: The Gnosis of Angels, Dreams, and Resurrection* (1996). *The Anxiety of Influence* (1973) sets forth Professor Bloom's provocative theory of the literary relationships between the great writers and their predecessors. His most recent books include *Shakespeare: The Invention of the Human*, a 1998 National Book Award finalist, and *How to Read and Why*, which was published in 2000.

Professor Bloom earned his Ph.D. from Yale University in 1955 and has served on the Yale faculty since then. He is a 1985 MacArthur Foundation Award recipient, served as the Charles Eliot Norton Professor of Poetry at Harvard University in 1987–88, and has received honorary degrees from the universities of Rome and Bologna. In 1999, Professor Bloom received the prestigious American Academy of Arts and Letters Gold Medal for Criticism.

Currently, Harold Bloom is the editor of numerous Chelsea House volumes of literary criticism, including the series BLOOM'S NOTES, BLOOM'S MAJOR DRAMATISTS, BLOOM'S MAJOR NOVELISTS, MAJOR LITERARY CHARACTERS, MODERN CRITICAL VIEWS, MODERN CRITICAL INTERPRETATIONS, and WOMEN WRITERS OF ENGLISH AND THEIR WORKS.

Editor's Note

My Introduction contrasts Lily Bart in *The House of Mirth* with Undine in *The Custom of the Country* and Ellen in *The Age of Innocence.*

As this volume includes over twenty-five views of these three novels and of *Ethan Frome*, I will confine myself here to remarks only upon a representative few.

Wai-Chee Dimock shrewdly notes that Lily Bart, protagonist of *The House of Mirth,* is trapped in the irony of paying for everything she does, in order to maintain her place in society, where non-payment is conformity. To be punished for following the rules is a Kafkan nightmare, and anticipates Lily's demise.

Ruth Bernard Yeazell ironically observes Lily's dilemma from a related perspective, observing that Lily must display herself, but also be modestly unnoticed. Lily dies because she lives both in Thorstein Veblen's city and in Old New York.

The narrator of *Ethan Frome* is judged by Cynthia Griffin Wolff to be a visionary of a ghastly sort, whose interpretation colors nearly everything we are told. This is very compatible with Candace Waid's perception that the narrator is haunted by images of infertility, and that his vision condemns the three protagonists to imprisonment in a living death.

Wharton's most unpleasant but most fascinating character, Undine Spragg in *The Custom of the Country,* is accurately seen by Gary H. Lindberg as an exception to the novelistic pattern in which an ascent in social class involves also some moral decay, as nothing seems capable of changing Undine. Claire Preston, in a related insight, classifies Undine with placeless Americans, always on the move, never arriving.

Margaret B. McDowell focuses upon Newland Archer's limitations in *The Age of Innocence*, showing that he underestimates May, whom he marries, and Ellen Olenska, whom he loves. The menace that Ellen represents to Old New York is stated by Carol Wershoven in terms that recognize one of Wharton's deepest ironies, that only Ellen takes seriously the mottoes of New York society. Ellen's intense individuality unfits her for Old New York, which cannot accept her internal strength, according to Kathy A. Fedorko, who rightly attributes self-reliance to Wharton's most engaging heroine.

Introduction

HAROLD BLOOM

Edith Wharton's three principal women characters—Lily Bart, Undine Spragg, Ellen Olenska—are remarkably varied, though Lily and Ellen both are motherless members of Old New York society, and Undine is an outsider who conquers and destroys that society, on her own egregious terms. Lily, though she struggles tenaciously, is finally too weak to survive the contradictions between her upbringing and her situation. It is Ellen, superbly self-reliant, who reconciles her heritage and her dilemmas, and who evokes our admiration. Lily dies of a sleeping-drug overdose; Undine, the American answer to Thackeray's Becky Sharp, holds on unpleasantly in our memory; while Ellen, who has affinities to Henry James's Isabel Archer, in *The Portrait of a Lady*, declines Isabel's example, and flourishes (so far as we know) apart from the dying society of Old New York, in which Edith Wharton had been raised.

I once was outrageous enough to ask a group of students whom they would choose—either to love or to be—among Lily, Undine, and Ellen, and was startled by their consensus, which was Undine, since sensibly I had expected Ellen to be their answer. Since I knew that they also had read *Vanity Fair,* I protested that Becky Sharp was charming if unsettling, but that Undine frightened me. She did not dismay them, whereas Lily's ill luck depressed them, and Ellen they felt was rather too good to be true. Perhaps Wharton, a powerful ironist, would have appreciated their choice, but to an archaic Romantic like myself, it came as a considerable surprise, or as another instance of what my mentor, Frederick A. Pottle, had called shifts of sensibility.

Undine, I protested lamely, was bad news, but they forgave her vulgarity (as Wharton could not) and one of them accurately indicated that the novel's famous conclusion was now seriously outdated:

> "Oh, that reminds me—" instead of obeying her he unfolded the paper. "I brought it in to show you something. Jim Driscoll's been appointed Ambassador to England."
> "Jim Driscoll—!" She caught up the paper and stared at the paragraph he pointed to. Jim Driscoll—that pitiful nonentity, with his stout mistrustful commonplace wife! It seemed extraordinary that the government should have

hunted up such insignificant people. And immediately she had a great vague vision of the splendours they were going to—all the banquets and ceremonies and precedences . . .

"I shouldn't say she'd want to, with so few jewels— " She dropped the paper and turned to her husband. "If you had a spark of ambition, that's the kind of thing you'd try for. You could have got it just as easily as not!"

He laughed and thrust his thumbs in his waistcoat armholes with the gesture she disliked. "As it happens, it's about the one thing I couldn't."

"You couldn't? Why not?"

"Because you're divorced. They won't have divorced Ambassadresses."

"They won't? Why not, I'd like to know?"

"Well, I guess the court ladies are afraid there'd be too many pretty women in the Embassies," he answered jocularly.

She burst into an angry laugh, and the blood flamed up into her face. "I never heard of anything so insulting!" she cried, as if the rule had been invented to humiliate her.

There was a noise of motors backing and advancing in the court, and she heard the first voices on the stairs. She turned to give herself a last look in the glass, saw the blaze of rubies, the glitter of her hair, and remembered the brilliant names on her list.

But under all the dazzle a tiny black cloud remained. She had learned that there was something she could never get, something that neither beauty nor influence nor millions could ever buy for her. She could never be an Ambassador's wife; and as she advanced to welcome her first guests she said to herself that it was the one part she was really made for.

In our current political climate, Undine could well be appointed an ambassador, and thus transcend being an Ambassador's wife. It is eighty-eight years since the publication of *The Custom of the Country*, and I have met Undine many times, here and abroad, in the universities, the media, and among diplomats. Wharton may have rendered Undine Spragg with a vividness beyond authorial intention. One remembers Lily Bart for her brave pathos, and Ellen Olenska for her decency and vitality. But Undine Spragg is one of the great white sharks of literature: dangerous, distasteful, and yet permanently valid as a representation of reality. ✣

Biography of
Edith Wharton

Edith Newbold Jones Wharton was born on January 24, 1862, in New York City. Her parents, George Frederic Jones (d. 1882) and Lucretia Rhinelander Jones (d. 1901), were descended from aristocratic New York families; like many of the families in Wharton's fiction, the Jones did not work for an income, but were able to live off of accumulated wealth. Wharton's two brothers were teenagers when she was born, so she essentially grew up as an only child. Her family traveled every year; they split their time between New York, Europe, and Newport (Rhode Island). Wharton made her society debut in 1878, when she was seventeen. In the same year, her first collection of poetry, *Verses,* was published, and one of her poems appeared in the *Atlantic Monthly.*

In 1885, Wharton married Edward "Teddy" Wharton, a man thirteen years her senior. The marriage was rocky, however, and Wharton suffered severe bouts of depression throughout the 1890s. She nonetheless managed to publish her first collection of short stories, *The Greater Inclination,* in 1899. Her first novel, *The Touchstone,* appeared in 1900. A longer novel, *The Valley of Decision,* followed in 1902; in the same year, the Whartons moved into "The Mount," a house in western Massachusetts designed by Wharton. She continued writing, publishing either a novel or collection of stories nearly every year. The critical and popular reception of *The House of Mirth* established Wharton as one of the foremost novelists of the early twentieth century. *Ethan Frome* appeared in 1911, followed by *The Reef* in 1912.

In Paris in 1907, Wharton met Morton Fullerton, an American journalist with whom she became close. They had a love affair for about two years, and in 1913, Wharton filed for divorce from her husband. In the same year, she published *The Custom of the Country.* Single and permanently residing in Paris, Wharton became dedicated to the Allied cause, and published a collection of pro-French propaganda essays, titled *Fighting France* and *The Book of the Homeless.* She returned to fiction in 1917 with *Summer,* followed by *The Marne* in 1918, and *The Age of Innocence* in 1920. In 1921, Wharton was awarded the Pulitzer Prize for *The Age of Innocence.* She received an honorary degree from Yale University in 1923, and the occasion marks her last visit to the United States. She spent the rest of her life in Paris, continuing to write. She published her memoirs, *A Backward Glance,* in 1934, and was at work on another novel, *The Buccaneers,* when she suffered a stroke and died on August 11, 1937. Wharton was buried in the Cimitiere des Gonards in Versailles, France. ❀

Plot Summary of
The House of Mirth

Book One of *The House of Mirth* opens in Grand Central Station in New York City. Lily Bart is on her way to visit Mr. and Mrs. Gus Trenor at the their estate, Bellomont, but she misses her train. She sees an acquaintance, Lawrence Selden, and they walk to his apartment in *The Benedick* to have tea while Lily waits for the next train. Lily and Selden are able to speak freely with one another because there is no possibility of a marriage between the two; with Selden, Lily is able to let down her social veneer and act naturally. Lily is twenty-nine years old, unmarried, and beautiful; she holds a respected place in New York society, but realizes that she is getting too old to continue to hold her position as an unmarried, marriageable society girl: "I've been about too long—people are getting tired of me; they are beginning to say I ought to marry." Although she has been "on the market" for eleven years, Lily has not succeeded in marrying. She has had many opportunities, but seems always to "sabotage" potential marriages before they are complete. Lily has been raised to be a society wife; she has no choice but to marry, and although she spends her time making herself available, there seems to be something in Lily that prevents her from following through. Lily's dilemma is therefore similar to Ellen Olenska's, Undine Spragg's, and even Ethan Frome's: what can a person do if they are unable to fulfill the role expected of them in society?

After two hours with Selden, Lily realizes she must run in order to catch her train. She hopes to leave the building unnoticed, as it is improper for an unmarried girl to spend time alone with a bachelor, but on the stairs of *The Benedick,* she passes a charwoman who stares at her. As she exits the building, she sees Simon Rosedale, a Jewish businessman recently successful in the New York business community. Although he is tolerated because of his wealth and business influence, Rosedale is not socially accepted by Lily's set. He implies that Lily is leaving a clandestine encounter. She snubs him, and hurries to the station.

At Bellomont, Lily's relative poverty interferes with the entertainment; if she loses money at cards, she is broke. We learn that Lily's father was financially ruined when she was nineteen years old. He died soon after, and Lily and her mother spent the next two years living with relatives, attempting to maintain appearances despite their poverty. Mrs. Bart died when Lily was twenty-one, and Lily's aunt, Mrs. Peniston, took her in. Mrs. Peniston is very rich, but she is unaware of the expense of Lily's lifestyle; Lily is always low on money. She "longed to drop out of the race and make an independent life for herself. But what manner of life would it be? She knew that she hated dinginess as much as her mother had hated it. . . ."

Lily spends her first day at Bellomont with Percy Gryce, a wealthy bachelor she hopes to marry. When Selden arrives, there is talk of an affair between him and Bertha Dorset; Lily is unexpectedly jealous. She is captivated by Selden's disdain for Society, and his seeming ability to function outside of it. She spends the day with Selden rather than Gryce; the pair take a long walk that afternoon. Selden mocks Lily's shallowness in looking only to marry money, and Lily resents his criticism: "Why do you make the things I have chosen seem hateful to me, if you have nothing to give me instead?" Selden is not wealthy enough to maintain Lily's standard of living, and Lily has been raised to expect a more luxurious lifestyle than the one Selden would be able to give her.

When they return to the house, they discover that Percy Gryce returned to New York. Judy berates Lily for ignoring him; he left because Bertha Dorset told him that Lily was a compulsive gambler. Surprisingly, Lily is not particularly upset. She offers to pick up Judy's husband, Gus, at the train station; she complains to him about her lack of funds, and he offers to invest her money in the stock market. Desperately needing money, Lily agrees.

Back in New York, Lily's investments have profited. Gus "pays" Rosedale for his business tips by helping integrate him into respectable society; he asks Lily to be polite to him. She is embarrassed, for Selden witnesses her faked politeness to Rosedale; this is the type of social hypocrisy that Selden despises, and Lily is conscious of somehow letting him down.

In her aunt's house, Lily meets the charwoman who stared at her in *The Benedick*. Mrs. Haffen, now employed by Mrs. Peniston, remembers Lily, and tries to sell her a stack of letters stolen from Selden's apartment; they were written by Bertha Dorset to Selden, and prove that they had an affair. Remembering Lily's unsupervised visit to Selden's apartment, Mrs. Haffen assumes that she is the writer of the letters, and thinks she is blackmailing Lily. Lily remembers Bertha's spitefulness in ruining her marriage to Gryce; she decides to buy the letters in order to revenge herself on Bertha.

The Wellington Brys throw a "general entertainment" at which Lily poses in one of the *tableaux vivants*. Selden is also at the party; they walk together in the garden and kiss, and Selden confesses his love for Lily. She is frightened of the ramifications of a romance with him, and leaves.

The next day, dining at Mrs. Fisher's, Gus convinces Lily to come to his townhouse to see his wife. But Judy is out of town, and Gus tries to force Lily into a sexual relationship with him in return for his financial help. Lily escapes, and flees to Selden's cousin Gerty's house. Gerty Farish has always been kind, and even though she is jealous of Lily because Selden loves her, Gerty welcomes and calms her. Lily realizes that she can no longer take money from Gus, and must repay her monetary debt to him as soon as possible. She asks her aunt for the money, but is refused. Rosedale calls on Lily, and asks her to marry him; she asks for time to think about it, and waits for Selden, who is supposed to visit that afternoon. But Selden never arrives. The night before, he tried to intercept Lily at Mrs. Fisher's, but Lily had already left with Gus when he arrived. Later, while taking a walk, he saw Lily leaving Gus's house, and assumed that they were having an affair. Unaware that Selden saw her, Lily is upset when she learns that he left the country the day before without calling on her.

Book Two opens in Monte Carlo. Lily has been traveling with the Dorsets and Ned Silverton (who is having an affair with Bertha Dorset). George discovers his wife's affair with Ned; he is furious, and sees Selden about getting a divorce. Bertha refuses to confide in Lily, and rather than discussing her own affair, Bertha criticizes Lily for behaving too familiarly with George. Lily is shocked, but forgives Bertha, understanding the stress she must be under. That night, the Dorsets, Lily, and Selden dine at the Brys. After dinner, Bertha "cuts" Lily; she publicly announces that Lily is no longer welcome on board her yacht. The suggestion, of course, is that Lily is having an affair with Bertha's husband; this public announcement effectively ruins Lily's position as a respectable society lady.

In New York, Mrs. Peniston dies and disinherits Lily in favor of her cousin, Grace Stepney; Lily inherits only 10,000 dollars, which she will not receive for some time. Grace refuses to loan Lily money, claiming that Lily's scandalous behavior in Monte Carlo caused her aunt's illness and death. Lily's old friends snub her; only Gerty Farish and Carry Fisher remain friendly. Mrs. Fisher, a quasi-respectable society lady, introduces her to the Gormer set; Lily is forced to integrate herself into a society group that she despised before her ruin. Mrs. Fisher also suggests that Lily marry as soon as possible; she suggests either George Dorset (pending his divorce from Bertha), or Rosedale.

While Lily is staying with Mattie Gormer on Long Island, she sees George Dorset. He apologizes for his wife's behavior, and asks Lily to marry him. She proudly refuses and returns to Mattie's house, where she sees Bertha leaving. Lily is (rightly) frightened that Bertha is now trying to ruin her in her new set. She calls on Rosedale and tells him that she will marry him. Rosedale refuses. Although he does seem to have a genuine affection for Lily, Rosedale's interest in her has always been linked to her social position; he wanted to marry her because it would help make him more respectable. But marrying Lily now would hurt his social standing. He suggests that Lily use Bertha's letters to Selden to blackmail Bertha into being friendly to her; if Bertha would readmit Lily into her set, then Rosedale would marry her.

Lily refuses to blackmail Bertha, and is slowly rejected by the Gormer set (due to Bertha's influence). At Gerty's request, Selden visits Lily, and discovers that she is now working as a social secretary for a vulgar but wealthy divorcée, Mrs. Norma Hatch. Selden tries to help her, but Lily refuses what she sees as charity.

Lily's leaves the service of Mrs. Hatch, and at Gerty's suggestion, takes a job in a millinery factory. She is ill and cannot sleep; her doctor gives her a prescription for chloral, a sleeping drug. The druggist warns her not to take too much because of the danger of overdose.

Lily is soon fired from the millinery shop. Rosedale visits her and offers to loan her the money to repay Gus Trenor; Lily refuses. Rosedale renews his conditional offer of marriage, and the next day, Lily decides to use Bertha's letters. On her way to confront Bertha, she passes *The Benedick,* and impulsively visits Selden. She apologizes to Selden, presumably an advance apology for using his letters to blackmail Bertha. But as Lily leaves the apartment, she realizes that she is morally unable to blackmail Bertha. Lily burns the letters.

Resting on a park bench, Lily is approached by Nettie Struther, a poor woman Lily once helped by donating money to Gerty's charitable society. Nettie recognizes Lily, and invites her to warm up in her apartment. Lily meets Nettie's child and husband, and is kindly received into their kitchen. When Lily returns to her boardinghouse, she receives a check for 10,000 dollars, her full inheritance from her aunt. Although she could use the money to reestablish herself in society, her pride forces her first to pay her debt to Gus. She feels very ill, and takes an extra does of chloral to help her sleep, seeing sleep as more important that the slight danger of overdose. She falls asleep.

The next morning, Selden visits Lily's boardinghouse to tell her that he loves her. He finds Gerty at the boardinghouse; Lily is dead. Gerty gives Selden thirty minutes alone with Lily's body before the doctor comes. Selden finds the check to Gus, and realizes that Lily's morals eventually superseded her desire to exist in respectable society. He regrets that he did not come to her sooner, and the novel ends with a suggestion that somehow Selden and Lily are able to reconcile after her death. ❀

List of Characters in
The House of Mirth

Lily Bart is the main character in the novel. She is a respected and beautiful society lady, but doesn't have the money to maintain the lifestyle. The plot revolves around her attempts, and failure, to marry a wealthy man.

Lawrence Selden has had an affair with Bertha Dorset, as proved by the letters Mrs. Haffen sells to Lily. He and Lily love each other, and one of the plots of the novel is their unsuccessful attempt to negotiate a marriage between them with their social obligations and expectations.

Gerty Farish, Selden's cousin, is poor and works for a living. She is very kind, and is in love with Selden. Although she knows he is in love with Lily, she is kind and helpful to Lily. Lily detests the life Gerty leads at the beginning of the novel, only to work with Gerty by the end.

Mrs. George Dorset (**Bertha**) tells Percy Gryce negative (and untrue) things about Lily, making him change his mind about marrying her. She has an affair with Ned Silverton, and publicly insinuates that Lily is in love with her husband, thus ruining Lily's respectability.

George Dorset is in love with Lily, and proposes marriage to her (dependent on his divorce from his adulterous wife, Bertha).

Mr. Simon Rosedale, the Jewish banker, is shunned by society because he is Jewish and new money, and grudgingly accepted because of his wealth. When the stock market crashes, Rosedale is one of the few who profits. He wants to marry Lily in order to complete his assimilation into society, but then refuses to marry her after her social ruin.

Gus Trenor offers to help Lily invest her money in the stock market, and in return, expects her to have an affair with him.

Mrs. Gus Trenor (**Judy**), a friend of Lily's, snubs her after her social ruin. Her husband, Gus, wants to have an affair with Lily.

Mrs. Peniston, Lily's aunt, raised her after her parents' death. In her will, she disinherits Lily in favor of Grace Stepney.

Ned Silverton, a poet and a gambler, has an affair with Bertha Dorset. In order to hide this affair, Bertha "sacrifices" Lily.

Mrs. Carry Fisher helps Lily after she is snubbed by society. She is a bit unorthodox: she has had two divorces, and is looked down upon by high society (including Lily before her social ruin).

Grace Stepney, an obscure cousin of Lily, inherits Mrs. Peniston's money, and tells Lily that her aunt died from worry because of Lily's gambling debts and scandalous behavior in Monte Carlo.

Mrs. Haffen is the charwoman at *The Benedick*, Selden's building. She brings Lily some of Selden and Bertha's letters that prove they had an affair. She threatens to reveal Lily's afternoon visit to Selden's room unless Lily buys the letters from her.

Mattie Gormer is the central figure of the social set that temporarily accepts Lily after her social ruin. Lily had previously looked down upon them; they eventually snub her as well.

Norma Hatch is a "rich, helpless, unplaced" divorcée living in New York. She hires Lily as her secretary, and supports her in the Emporium Hotel.

Nettie (Crane) Struther has been a beneficiary of one of Gerty's charitable societies. During her involvement with the charities, Lily has helped Nettie recover from an illness. Nettie repays the kindness by inviting Lily up to her small apartment to meet her daughter, who is named for an actress who looks like Lily. ❀

Critical Views on
The House of Mirth

[Diana Trilling (1905–1996) was a literary critic for *The Nation* and *The New Yorker*. She published several volumes of collected essays and reviews (*Reviewing the Forties*, 1975), and a memoir, *The Beginning of the Journey*. Here, Trilling discusses the "historical moment" of *The House of Mirth*.]

At the turn of the century, which is the period of *The House of Mirth*, Mrs. Wharton's social class had already begun to feel the assaults that in our own day have spelled the disappearance of its once-unquestioned sense of power. Inherited wealth had begun to capitulate to new financial success; infiltrations from an uneasy European aristocracy and from the freer lands of the theater and art had already presaged our present-day international set. The solvent was at work within even the innermost circles of hereditary privilege, preparing the democratic integration and the mobility between classes with which we are now familiar.

One counts several carefully differentiated strata of New York Society in Mrs. Wharton's novel—the Proustian precision with which these dividing lines are drawn is not the least of the fascinations of the book. But it is not so much in their differences—the fact, say, that the Dorset-Trenor circle takes it for granted that ladies smoke and gamble, while the Gryce-Van Osburgh-Peniston circle countenances no such impropriety—as in their shared weaknesses that we read the impending collapse of the whole precious structure. If the conservatives of Society feel threatened by Dorsets and Trenors who no longer adhere to the rules by which they were reared, these "faster" members of their class are similarly aware of the new forces beating at *their* gate and the new values to which they are soon to be exposed; no segment of Society but knows it is imperiled by the large movement of social change. And although in isolated personal instances there may be a certain flexibility in response to the disturbance of old patterns, there is no class flexibility with which to accommodate a new order. Nor is there, of course, an adequate inflexibility or intransigence with which to resist it; there cannot be, unless this world of privilege marshal its strength to destroy the insurgent democratic horde—an act of militant counter-assertion, actually of counter-revolution, which society is already too decadent even to envision. What Mrs. Wharton is describing, in other words, is the inexorable process of history as it worked itself out in the America with which she was best acquainted.

An artist fiercely in possession of her own particular materials, Mrs. Wharton only once—and this once rather deplorably—undertakes to introduce into her novel the encroaching democratic mass which constitutes the palpable or, at any rate, the ultimate social enemy. This is when Lily Bart, nearing the climax of her short career, encounters a working-class girl whose path she had crossed in a vagrant moment of personal philanthropy. For the rest, Mrs. Wharton's representative of the new social dispensation is a Jew, a very rich Jew, Simon Rosedale, who is intent upon making a marriage which will fittingly ornament his enormous wealth and ensure him a place in Society. Not only the innermost circles but even the outlying sections of the old aristocratic world are at first resistant to Rosedale's intrusion; but they are unable to withstand the power of his money, and his urgency of personal ambition. This most alien of Mrs. Wharton's characters at last penetrates the central strongholds; and if his worldly success coincides with the steady revelation of a far more feeling nature than showed in the days when he was failing so dismally in his social effort, we can take this as not the least pointed of Mrs. Wharton's comments on the connection between social realities and the life of the emotions. Obviously Mrs. Wharton is not saying that an achieved position in Society is the warrant of good feelings: her panorama of Lily's brutally shallow and callous friends argues quite the opposite. But she surely is saying that our gentler emotions have a hard time thriving when we lack a sense of our secure niche in the world, whatever it may be, or, as in Lily's case, without the nourishment of money.

The historical moment, then, of *The House of Mirth* is the moment when a Jew—and a self-made Jew at that, uncouth and charmless, whose deviations from accepted deportment are as conspicuous as his wealth and as grating on the sensitive nerve of Society—can aspire to associate on equal terms with the old Hudson Valley families. But this is still the moment when the old social monarchs, aware that a new dynasty of wealth storms the inherited realm, cling most tenaciously to their rights of blood; the struggle is the fiercer because eventually so futile. Through most of *The House of Mirth* Rosedale takes social and personal insult to a degree that would flatten any except a man of iron will—except a man, that is, whose personal will was synonymous with the will of history. His strength of endurance lies in his awareness that it is only so long as the old fortunes hold out that the old families can maintain their prestige and power, and in his sure knowledge that his own shrewd speculations on Wall Street are in the process of blasting their hereditary fortress.

—Irving Howe, ed., *Edith Wharton: A Collection of Critical Essays* (Englewood Cliffs: Prentice-Hall, Inc., 1962): pp. 106–8.

CYNTHIA GRIFFIN WOLFF ON SELDEN'S IMPOSSIBLE STANDARD

> [Cynthia Griffin Wolff is the Class of 1922 Professor of Literature at the Massachusetts Institute of Technology. In addition to editing the Norton edition of *Ethan Frome,* she published *A Feast of Words: The Triumph of Edith Wharton,* and *Emily Dickinson.* Here she discusses Selden's expectations of Lily, and the way Lily's belief in them causes her fall.]

Given the entirely dependent nature of Lily's sense of self, we can understand Selden's importance to her: his critical stance adds a moral dimension to her life; for although she has repeatedly succeeded in confirming her effect as a merely decorative object, she has found this success insufficient. Thus intimacy between Lily and Selden involves her adopting his point of view, submitting to his judgments. And his judgment is generally harsh. "That was the secret of his way of readjusting her vision. Lily, turning her eyes from him, found herself scanning her little world through his retina: it was as though the pink lamps had been shut off and the dusty daylight let in." Yet, as we have seen, his own moral-aesthetic code is deeply flawed. It is a code that even he can follow only by a series of suppressed hypocrisies: he is as much a parasite on the society of the House of Mirth as Lily is—she timidly points this fact out, but has not the internal stamina and coherence to pursue her point; his affair with Bertha Dorset scarcely justifies the chaste horror he manifests at the possibility that Lily's conduct has been less that absolutely perfect. In submerging her ethical view into his, Lily has accepted impossible standards.

There is, however, an even more seriously destructive element in Selden's system as applied to Lily: it continues the process by which society has dehumanized her. Selden is willing to judge her worthy if and only if she can become a flawless, absolutely constant embodiment of virtue. When Lily accepts his unattainable ideals as her "realities," she is merely perpetuating on a somewhat loftier plane the lifelong habit of seeing herself as an object to be judged by others. In her relationship to Selden "she longed to be to him something more than a piece of sentient prettiness, a passing diversion to his eye and brain," but she evokes from him little more than ironic, detached disapproval. And since she has accepted the notion that his reactions are the only "mirror" in which her "real" self can be reflected, she perceives that self as increasingly disgusting and loathsome. Each episode of gentle admonition on his part is a blow. "She looked at him helplessly, like a hurt or frightened child: this real self of hers, which he had the faculty of drawing out of the depths, was so little accustomed to go alone." Little wonder that she does not think of loving him; that act would require an independent identity. Instead her needs are expressed in terms that plead for his reassuring response: "It seemed to her that it was for him only she cared to be beautiful."

The artificial quality of Lily's one great success—her impersonation of Reynolds's portrait—indicates the impossibility of sustaining Selden's idealized image on any but an otherworldly level. Thus afterwards she sighs, "'Ah, love me, love me—but don't tell me so!'"

Lily's acceptance of Selden's demands on her renders her even less able than before to return to the moral lassitude of an easier environment. "The renewed habit of luxury—the daily waking to an assured absence of care and presence of material ease—gradually blunted her appreciation of these values, and left her more conscious of the void they could not fill." When Selden visits here at Mrs. Hatch's apartment, Lily is conscious of her emotional need for an expression of feeling on his part; but when he proffers only cold, cruel judgment, she is incapable of resisting her revulsion from the "real self " that his criticism seems once more to have uncovered. The narrator repeatedly suggests that "the situation between them was one which could have been cleared up only by a sudden explosion of feeling." But the habits of a lifetime cannot be dismissed. Selden has been formed as connoisseur, Lily as collectable; "their whole training and habit of mind were against the chances of such an explosion." Lily must persist to the end with the only roles she understands, and her final preoccupation becomes the reclamation of "self " in Selden's eyes—at no matter what cost. The significance of her death becomes clearer when we define her dilemma in this way. We can never know whether it was a conscious act; so many of her finer gestures seem acts of carelessness, of thoughtless inattention. Yet the effect of her death is redemptive: it recaptures and fixes forever Selden's esteem for her; it apotheosizes her triumphant *tableau vivant.*

—Cynthia Griffin Wolff, *A Feast of Words: The Triumph of Edith Wharton* (New York: Oxford UP, 1977): pp. 129–131.

WAI-CHEE DIMOCK ON LILY'S RELATION TO THE MARKETPLACE

[Wai-chee Dimock is Professor of English at Yale University. She has published *Residues of Justice: Literature, Law, Philosophy,* and *Empire for Liberty: Melville and the Poetics of Imagination.* Here she examines the ways in which Lily both mirrors, and rebels against, the marketplace.]

It is not Selden but Lily, the woman he tutors and scolds, who comes closest to breaking away from the rules and premises of the marketplace. Lily is also, of course, the only one who pays routinely and scrupulously, and often with currency she can little afford. "You think we live *on* the rich, rather than with them," Lily observes to

Gerty, "and so we do, in a sense—but it's a privilege we have to pay for!" She is right. It is no accident that the one who pays most regularly is also the one with the scantest means, for nonpayment, as we have seen, is a privilege of the powerful, those who fix the rate of exchange. Lily is therefore the obverse of, and the needed complement to, three characters: Bertha Dorset, who avoids paying by making others foot the bill; Mrs. Peniston, who scrimps on her obligations; and Lawrence Selden, who pulls out when the deal seems overly risky. "Paying" is Lily's habitual way of being, and she is at it almost as soon as the book opens. It is she, not Selden, who has to "pay so dearly for" her visit to his apartment. Lily goes on to pay for her stay at Bellomont by performing "social drudgery" for Mrs. Trenor as well as by incurring gambling debts. She pays for her momentary truancy from Percy Gryce. She pays Trenor, though not to his satisfaction. She pays Bertha for the cruise on the *Sabrina*, just as she pays Norma Hatch for her brief stay at the Emporium Hotel. And she pays, finally, for those extravagant sentiments she permits herself to feel toward Selden.

Lily's dutiful payments are altogether in keeping with the principle of exchange. She is merely doing what the system requires of her, what she is supposed to. And yet—such is the irony of exchange—it is precisely this strict compliance that marks her as a deviant. Lily is working, after all, within a system in which nonpayment is the norm, in which violation is the only mode of conformity. She is penalized, then, not for breaking the rules but for observing them. This sort of absurdity is the logic of nightmare, but it is just this absurd logic that makes the exchange system work. In its disfiguring light Lily's "rebellion" takes on the correspondingly absurd form of playing by the rules, of rebellion by submission.

Lily's paradoxical conformity and deviance come across most clearly in her dealings with Trenor. Having taken almost nine thousand dollars from him and finding her obligation "not the sort . . . one could remain under," she proceeds to settle her debt as soon as she receives her aunt's legacy—a decision that "cleans [her] out altogether," as Rosedale rather indelicately puts it. In repaying Trenor, Lily is indeed complying with the rules of exchange, but she is also challenging the very basis of exchange. Trenor never expects to be paid back in quite this way. "Payment in kind," the most primitive form of barter economy, has no place in a highly developed social marketplace, which trades on the putative equivalence between disparate entities. By paying back the exact monetary amount, by equating nine thousand dollars with nine thousand dollars, Lily at once obeys the principle of exchange and reduces it to tautology. Her nine-thousand-dollar debt is now just that: a nine-thousand-dollar debt, not some ill-defined and possibly limitless obligation. In other words, by making money its own equivalent, Lily reduces it to its own terms and defies its purchasing power. She has understood what it means to live under the "intolerable obligation" of an all-consuming system of exchange, and she now tries to exorcise its influence by facing up to what she owes—in all the crudeness and brutality of its cash amount—just to rescue from its dominion the other strands of her life. What appears as a gesture of submission turns out to be a gesture of defiance, for by adhering literally to the terms of exchange Lily turns the system on its head. And yet, as every reader must recognize, defiance of this sort is ultimately unavailing. The exchange system can easily accommodate rebellion like Lily's: Trenor, no doubt, will take the money and even circulate it anew. Lily's action hurts no one but herself. It remains a challenge to the exchange system in spirit but not in fact.

—Wai-chee Dimock, "Debasing Exchange: Edith Wharton's *House of Mirth*," *PMLA* 100, no. 5 (October 1985): pp. 787–788.

RUTH BERNARD YEAZELL ON "OLD" NEW YORK

[Ruth Bernard Yeazell is Professor of English and Chair of the English Department at Yale University. She is the author of *Language and Knowledge in the Late Novels of Henry James* and *Fictions of Modesty: Women and Courtship in the English Novel*. Here she examines the similarities between "old" and "new" New York through the characters of Mrs. Peniston and Bertha Dorset.]

Well before Bertha Dorset accuses Lily of having been "so conspicuously" alone with George Dorset late at night in Monte Carlo, Grace Stepney begins to alienate Mrs. Peniston from her niece by passing on rumors that have been circulating about the latter's relation to

Gus Trenor. "People always say unpleasant things," she remarks with a complacent sense of her worldly superiority to Mrs. Peniston, "— and certainly they're a great deal together," she adds maliciously. "It's a pity Lily makes herself so conspicuous."

> "*Conspicuous!*" gasped Mrs. Peniston. She bent forward, lowering her voice to mitigate the horror. "What sort of things do they say? That he means to get a divorce and marry her?"
>
> Grace Stepney laughed outright. "Dear me, no! He would hardly do that. It—it's a flirtation—nothing more."
>
> "A flirtation? Between my niece and a married man?"

Wharton makes clear that this is old New York speaking—and that the closed and comparatively small town of Mrs. Peniston's girlhood is rapidly disappearing into the speed and crowds of the modern city. Significantly enough, Mrs. Peniston never figures in those large throngs of spectators who gaze admiringly on her niece. Indeed, so far as we can tell, she scarcely ever ventures beyond her drawing-room, where she keeps her imagination as "shrouded," the narrator suggests, as the furniture. Yet Mrs. Peniston too of course is a watcher—a "looker-on at life" whose mind has earlier been figured as "one of those little mirrors which her Dutch ancestors were accustomed to affix to their upper windows, so that from the depths of an impenetrable domesticity they might see what was happening in the street." Her New York has no rush hours at Grand Central Station, in other words, just those village-like streets into which her niece keeps stepping at awkward moments, streets whose only occupant proves always, however implausibly, someone she knows. Caught between the imperative to display herself and the injunction to keep herself modestly out of sight, Lily dies, one might say, partly because she lives both in Veblen's city and Mrs. Peniston's.

In the later chapters of *The House of Mirth*, and in occasional retrospective remarks on the novel to others, Wharton sometimes evokes its Old New York with a certain incongruous nostalgia—as if by comparison to the spectacularly vulgar standards of the newest *nouveaux riches*, Mrs. Peniston's copy-book axioms had suddenly been converted into satisfactory guides to the moral life. "Compared with the vast gilded void of Mrs. Hatch's existence," for example, "the life of Lily's former friends seemed packed with ordered activities." Confronted with the multiply-divorced and very wealthy Mrs.

Hatch, who arrives from somewhere vaguely out West to swim "in a haze of indeterminate enthusiasms, of aspirations culled from the stage, the newspapers, the fashion-journals, and a gaudy world of sport," Lily suddenly discovers that "even the most irresponsible pretty woman of her acquaintance had her inherited obligations, her conventional benevolences, her share in the working of the great civic machine; and all hung together in the solidarity of these traditional functions". In an often-quoted valedictory passage, the narrator deplores Lily's "rootless and ephemeral" life, her lack of "grave endearing traditions" and a "centre of early pieties," implicitly comparing the House of Mirth to "the concrete image of the old house stored with visual memories, or . . . the conception of the house not built with hands, but made up of inherited passions and loyalties." Writing about the novel to the rector of New York's Trinity Church a few months after it was published, Wharton similarly appeared to suggest that her subject was the difference between the traditional loyalties of the old money and the rootlessness of the new: "Social conditions as they are just now in our new world, where the sudden possession of money has come without inherited obligations, or any traditional sense of solidarity between the classes, is a vast & absorbing field for the novelist." At such moments it is almost as if Wharton wanted to forget the collusion of old money and new that she had in fact represented, or as if she could somehow undo her heroine's fate by substituting a consoling image of the past for the world of "inherited obligations" she had already satirized in Mrs. Peniston.

> The most vivid thing about her was the fact that her grandmother had been a Van Alstyne. This connection with the well-fed and industrious stock of early New York revealed itself in the glacial neatness of Mrs. Peniston's drawing-room and in the excellence of her cuisine. She belonged to the class of old New Yorkers who have always lived well, dressed expensively, and done little else; and to these inherited obligations Mrs. Peniston faithfully conformed.

Wharton sometimes writes as if "the sudden possession of money" marked a great divide between this old world and the new, but she knows as well as Veblen himself that the leisure class is an archaic institution. Mrs. Peniston might register shock at Mrs. Dorset's gambling, not to mention her adulteries, but both women recognize an obligation to live well and dress expensively; and from beyond the grave, as we have seen, the older woman reenacts the younger one's cut of Lily.

—Ruth Bernard Yeazell, "The Conspicuous Wasting of Lily Bart," *ELH* 59 (1992): pp. 728–730.

EILEEN CONNELL ON THE SENTIMENTALITY OF NETTIE STRUTHER

[Eileen Connell is a former graduate student at the University of Virginia. She defended her dissertation, *The Age of Experience: Edith Wharton and the Divorce Question in Early Twentieth Century America.* Here, Connell focuses on the relationship between Nettie Struther and Lily Bart.]

Nettie looks up to Lily as a model of ideal feminine virtue and happiness who is "high up, where everything [is] just grand." But just as Lily's representation of Nettie is not the result of an objective investigation of the facts of her life as a poor working mother, Nettie beams at Lily with "exultation" because Lily represents her sentimental ideal of the beautiful, glamorous society lady she would like to be. When she "felt real mean," Nettie would remember that at least Lily was "having a wonderful time anyhow," and when she stopped seeing Lily's name in the papers she "began to be afraid [Lily] was sick" and almost became sick herself "fretting about it." Nettie even names her daughter after an actress who reminds her of Lily and hopes that the baby will "grow up just like [Lily]." Echoing the working girl who said "it was as good as a day in the country just to look at [Lily]," Nettie suggests that her image of Lily helped her as much as the trip to the vacation house. She tells Lily, "I only wish I could help *you*—but I suppose there's nothing else I could do."

She does help, of course, in the same way that Lily helps her—by exemplifying an admirable type of female identity. Nettie achieves what Lily does not, motherhood and the "strength to gather up the fragments of her life and build herself a shelter with them." While Wharton represents ironically Nettie's sentimental interpretation of Lily, who is neither "high up" or grand, she does not qualify Lily's idealization of this poor working girl. As many readers of this chapter have noted, Wharton's portrayal of Nettie Struther is unabashedly sentimental. She indulges freely here in clichés from sentimental novels and in the rhetoric of emotional excess. Nettie survives the worldly forces to which the heroine succumbs; her once ailing "frail envelope [is] now alive with hope and energy." Like the typical sentimental heroine, she achieves a reward for her "ceaseless labor of self-transformation." Just when she did not "have the heart to go on working for [her]self," she gets a husband, a baby, and a home. These apparently traditional rewards identify Nettie as an example of a sentimentalized "proud, independent, self-reliant, efficient" working girl.

Not surprisingly, many recent critics of *The House of Mirth* read the ending as a retreat from the novel's social criticism, reasoning that these "stock sentimental pieces" undercut the rest of the novel's critique of the position of the commodified woman in society. But the sentimental portrayal of Nettie Struther can be interpreted as part of, rather than a retreat from, the novel's social criticism if one considers that Wharton recuperates here the original function of sentimentalism. One of the goals of eighteenth-century sentimental fiction was to encourage its readers to identify emotionally and to sympathize with classes of characters formerly not represented in literature—the poor, animals, and children, for instance. As Philip Fisher observes, the "presence of sentimentality is most obvious . . . where new materials, new components of the self, new types of heroes and heroines, new subjects of mood and feeling occur." In *The House of Mirth,* representations of domesticity and of female subjectivity are formulated in an old style, but they offer innovative responses to the contemporary realities they expose.

—Eileen Connell, "Edith Wharton Joins the Working Classes: *The House of Mirth* and the New York City Working Girls' Clubs," *Women's Studies* 26 (October 1997): pp. 587–589.

[Bonnie Lynn Gerard is adjunct Professor of English at the University of North Texas. She has published several articles on such authors as Thomas Hardy and Elizabeth Gaskell. Here she discusses Lily's concept of being divided in two, focusing on her last meeting with Selden.]

⟨. . .⟩ Selden's love for her—his "belief" in her—has made it impossible that she sell herself entirely; her vague sense of her potential for moral depravity causes her to imagine that she can effectively divide herself into two parts, the material and the spiritual, and that she can act on the former while protecting the latter from implication. She says to Selden:

> There is some one I must say goodbye to. Oh, not *you*—we are sure to see each other again—but the Lily Bart you knew. I have kept her with me all this time, but now we are going to part, and I have brought her back to you—I am going to leave her here. When I go out presently she will not go with me. I shall like to think that she has stayed with you—and she'll be no trouble, she'll take up no room.

Such a rhetoric of division is convenient for Lily, except that only a few moments prior she had decided she must "make him understand that she had saved herself whole from the seeming ruin of her life," and that "he must see her wholly for once before they parted." Nowhere in the novel is the undercurrent of romantic neoplatonism as powerful as in this moment of Lily's final struggle for an undivided self. Animating neoplatonist writing from Plotinus to Hegel to Wordsworth is the tension between division, the defining quality of material existence, and wholeness, the spiritual state of undifferentiated unity. Lily wants Selden to see her wholly, but the problem is that she cannot see herself wholly in the first place. This is because, in appropriately romantic terms, to see herself wholly requires that Lily see herself as a being capable of love—not of being loved, but of loving. ⟨. . .⟩ The moment in which Lily becomes suddenly aware of her love for Selden—"something lived between them also, and leaped up in her like an imperishable flame: it was the love his love had kindled, the passion of her soul for his"—is the first time Lily truly knows herself in the novel. Consequently, the divided self is no longer possible: "that self" that she has discovered "must indeed live on in [Selden's] presence, but it must still continue to be hers." The moment is even figuratively sublime, for Lily intuits the truth of her feelings as if in the presence of a "light" around which "everything else dwindled and fell away from her."

To reinforce the sublimity of the moment, Wharton continues in the Pauline vein when she describes the effect of Lily's transformation on Selden: "he felt it only as one of those rare moments which lift the veil from their faces as they pass." The veil as symbol has a rich and varied history in literature and in literary criticism, and Wharton's use of it here is no less rich and complex. ⟨. . .⟩ For Wharton, too, the veil betokens an elusive alterity, the inscrutability of which may well be envisioned by Selden in feminine guise, much as Conrad's Jim, in another emblematically modern instance, imagines that "in the short moment of his last proud unflinching glance, he had beheld the face of that opportunity which, like an Eastern bride, had come veiled to his face." Jim's moment of romantic transcendence is not only feminized but orientalized as well, in a gesture that seems to undercut his romantic heroism by revealing an atavistic, selfish desire for possession of some radiant Other. For Wharton, the veil is similarly lifted to reveal a moment, but here it is a moment of intuited truth between Selden and Lily that is not only sublime but also mutual and sustaining. ⟨. . .⟩ Thus for Wharton, the lifted veil reveals the achievement of self-knowledge in a moment of sublime transcendence for both Lily and Selden, and as the old way of knowing passes, Selden is enabled to say of his rekindled love for Lily, "Things may change—but they don't pass."

—Bonnie Lynn Gerard, "From Tea to Chloral: Raising the Dead Lily Bart," *Twentieth Century Literature* 44, no. 4 (Winter 1998): pp. 419–421.

[Jennie A. Kassanoff is Assistant Professor of English at Barnard College. She has published several articles about Edith Wharton, including "Extinction, Taxidermy, Tableaux Vivants: Staging Race in *The House of Mirth*" and "Corporate Thinking: Edith Wharton's *The Fruit of the Tree*." Here she discusses Wharton's use of the "type," and the ways in which Lily escapes the stereotype of typing.]

The Bry entertainment opens with a series of tableaux "in which the fugitive curves of living flesh [. . .] have been subdued to plastic harmony without losing the charm of life." Wharton's socialite performers, accommodating themselves to the limitations of theatrical form, effectively become "types." Carry Fisher's "short dark-skinned face," for instance, makes a "typical Goya," while a "young Mrs. Van Alstyne, who showed the frailer Dutch type, [. . .] made a characteristic Vandyck." Such classifications participate in the novel's pervasive discourse of racial typology. Rosedale, for example, is earlier described as "a plump rosy man of the blond Jewish type," while Selden has "keenly-modelled dark features which, in a land of amorphous types, gave him the air of belonging to a more specialized race." A staple of Victorian vocabulary, *type*, indicated a distinct racial ontology of permanent (if often peculiar) genetic characteristics—a way of determining the general by extrapolating from the specific. ⟨. . .⟩

> [S]o skillfully had the personality of the actors been subdued to the scenes they figured in that even the least imaginative of the audience must have felt a thrill of contrast when the curtain suddenly parted on a picture which was simply and undisguisedly the portrait of Miss Bart.
>
> Here there could be no mistaking the predominance of personality—the unanimous "Oh!" of the spectators was a tribute, not to the brush-work of Reynolds's "Mrs. Lloyd" but to the flesh and blood loveliness of Lily Bart. [. . .] It was as though she had stepped, not out of, but into, Reynolds's canvas, banishing the phantom of his dead beauty by the beams of her living grace.

As an astonishingly vibrant portrait of herself, Lily cannot be reduced to type. Indeed, by choosing "a type so like her own that she could embody the person represented without ceasing to be herself," Lily transcends typology altogether: she effectively performs the impossible, subordinating the Galtonian composite to her personal specificity. Unlike her assimilating peers, Lily resists the generic abstraction of "plastic harmony," preserving instead her "flesh-and-blood loveliness." Were she to become the portrait she represents, she would risk losing the eugenic quality that makes her previous tableaux so arresting and racially loaded. She would risk, in short, becoming a mere type—either the equivalent of the racially typologized Jew or what Seltzer describes as "the American as typical, standard, and reproducible."

Wharton rescues Lily from these possibilities by stressing the "predominance of personality"—the "serious purity of the central conception" that can "break through the strongest armour of stock formulas." "Undisguisedly" herself, Lily stands in stylized opposition to the generic and the mechanized—a strategy not without risk. Throughout the novel, Wharton implies that Lily is imperiled by the very racial economy she represents—an economy consumed with purity and terrified of sham. Lily's embodiment of the William Jamesian double self—"there were two selves in her, the one she had always known, and a new abhorrent being to which it found itself chained"—crystallizes this vulnerability. Struggling to define her real self in a world where distinctions between the genuine and the imitative, the natural and the cultural have all but collapsed, Lily's crisis reveals the instability of race as an ontological category. Indeed, Wharton can only tenuously resolve this problem by shifting the grounds of the debate. To be a real self, she increasingly suggests, is to be realigned with a racial soul—the "slowly-accumulated past [that] lives in the blood." Walter Benn Michaels's contention that race in this period becomes essentially invisible—something spiritually inherited rather than physically acquired ("Souls")—is thus central to Wharton's logic. Hovering over Lily's deathbed, Selden fantasizes that he can distinguish the "sleeping face" from "the real Lily" who was "close to him, yet invisible and inaccessible." Only in her final tableau of death is Lily truly transmogrified into her authentic racial personality—a disembodied soul, at once real and invisible.

—Jennie A. Kassanoff, "Extinction, Taxidermy, Tableaux Vivants: Staging Race and Class in *The House of Mirth*," *PMLA* 115, no. 1 (January 2000): pp. 66–68.

CLAIRE PRESTON ON THE DARWINIAN FAILURE OF LILY BART

[Claire Preston is the Graduate Tutor in Sidney Sussex College, Cambridge University. She has edited a collection of works by Sir Thomas Browne, and published a critical study of Wharton, *Edith Wharton's Social Register*. Here she reads the story in naturalist terms, seeing Lily as a Darwinian failure.]

In her 1935 introduction to the Oxford University Press edition of *The House of Mirth*, Wharton spoke of 'the key' to the story in Darwinian metaphors:

> Nature, always apparently wasteful, and apparently compelled to create dozens of stupid people in order to produce a single genius, seems to reverse the process in manufacturing the shallow and the idle. Such groups always rest on an underpinning of wasted human possibilities; and it seemed to me that the fate of the persons embodying these possibilities ought to redeem my subject from insignificance.

The redeemed subject, Lily Bart, begins as one of the shallow and the idle, ends as part of the underpinning, the wasted element. The failure of her individual social ascent simultaneously traces her developing sense of the Darwinian ecosystem and her own insufficiency within it. Lily's circle offers her examples of how to dominate the competition in Bertha Dorset, how to abandon it in Selden, how to be spared it in Gerty Farish, how to survive it in Nettie Struther, and—her own experience—how to be overwhelmed by it, to have 'the sense of being swept like a stray uprooted growth down the heedless current of the years'. To comprehend these alternatives, *The House of Mirth* is couched in the jargon and concepts of competition and natural selection, and the beginnings of a realist social con-science (some of the themes of *The Fruit of the Tree,* her next full-length novel, are emerging). But the novel is not really concerned with the working classes: as Janet Flanner unkindly remarked, Wharton's writing about this group generally has the brittleness of a banker taking his typist to dine, 'a mere excursion out of one's class', and Nettie Struther is no more than a useful stereotype of plucky determination. In *The House of Mirth* those depths are evoked only to demonstrate from what a height *Lily* has fallen, and to attach pathos to that regression. 'You don't know what it's like', Lily tells Selden, 'in the rubbish heap!'

A specialised creature, 'an organism as helpless out of its narrow range as a sea-anemone torn from the rock', this analogy of Lily as biological failure recurs: she is oppressed by 'the feeling of being something rootless and ephemeral, mere spin-drift of the whirling surface of existence, without anything to which the poor little tenta-cles of self could cling before the awful flood submerged them'. Selden wonders presciently 'was it not possible that the material was fine, but that circumstance had fashioned it into a futile shape?' He imagines himself as amphibious and adaptable, able to exist in more than one environment; in fact, Selden is complacent, not a striver or a victor in any social, professional, or aesthetic contest. Lily's other serious suitor, Rosedale, is most adaptable of all, is 'not the man to waste his time in an ineffectual sentimental dalliance. He was too busy, too practical, and above all too much preoccupied with his own advancement, to indulge in such unprofitable asides'. Almost like the old Darwinian vignette of certain proto-pulmonary fishes casting themselves ashore, there to find that they can breathe and crawl across the beach with their rudimentary lungs and legs, Rosedale is seen dragging himself through the socio-genetic ranks toward the apex of power and dominion, 'working up' his social position. Lily, by contrast, seems able to contemplate *only* ineffectual sentimental dalliances which cannot further her aims, and may even damage them; moreover, she believes that her being can only 'dilate' in luxury, a climate and atmosphere for which she is specially evolved. She does seem, however, to possess certain useful adaptive abilities: her moods usually reflect her surroundings like the protec-tive coloration of certain animals; but this potentially useful modu-lation (Theodore Dreiser invokes it to explain Frank Cowperwood's immense success) actually exposes her: she tends—dangerously—to feel rich when surrounded by wealth, to be pointlessly dispirited by ugliness, to feel adventurous in risky situations; and these emotions usually lead her into difficulty, not safety. And she lacks real survival instincts: all her effects, although they seem spontaneous, are in fact carefully premeditated; her resourcefulness is merely illusory; and 'it was characteristic of her to feel that the only problems she could not solve were those with which she was not familiar'. The reed-like suppleness which a precarious existence has taught her, and has allowed her to bend with the prevailing social wind to maintain her foothold in the shifting social soil, crystallises during adversity into 'one hard, brilliant substance', a glassy unyielding finish which is more likely to crack and break than to bend. By her own admission bred to be ornamental rather than practical, Lily is merely 'very expensive', her 'vague wealth of . . . graces' not even as pragmatic as the hummingbird's bright plumage. The 'purely decorative mission', she realises near the end of her life, is even harder to carry out in society than in nature. In terms of survival, she fails to attract a viable mate, she will not reproduce herself, and she cannot succeed as a breadwinner.

—Claire Preston, *Edith Wharton's Social Register* (New York: St. Martin's Press, Inc., 2000): pp. 52–54.

Plot Summary of
Ethan Frome

The text opens as a first-person narrative. The speaker is unnamed, and is a visitor to Starkfield, Massachusetts, where the story takes place. In the Preface, the narrator introduces the reader to Ethan Frome. Frome is fifty-two years old, has a large red scar across his forehead, and he walks with "a lameness checking each step like the jerk of a chain." The narrator tells of his first encounter with Ethan, which occurred "several years" before the actual time of the Preface. He asks Harmon Gow about Ethan, and Gow tells him that Ethan is crippled because of a "smash-up" twenty-four years earlier.

But the narrator is not satisfied with Gow's explanation; he "had the sense that the deeper meaning of the story was in the gaps." The narrator is an engineer, sent to Massachusetts in order to work on a power-house at Corbury Junction, a nearby town. However, due to a carpenters' strike, the work is delayed and the narrator is forced to spend the winter in Starkfield, waiting for work to resume. He rents a room from Mrs. Ned Hale, a relatively wealthy widow. The narrator implies that she is somewhat of a gossip, but on the subject of Ethan Frome she became "unexpectedly reticent." Gow tells the narrator that Ruth Varnum (who became Mrs. Ned Hale) was "the first one to see 'em, after they was picked up. . . .The young folks was all friends, and I guess she just can't bear to talk about it."

The narrator claims that had it not been for "the accident of personal contact with the man," he might have been content with these fragments of Ethan's story. During his stay in Starkfield, the narrator drives daily to Corbury Flats with Denis Eady, the Irish grocer. Halfway through the winter, however, Eady's horses fall ill and the narrator is forced to find an alternate method of transport to the Flats. Gow suggests asking Ethan Frome, who agrees in order to earn extra money. For the next week, Frome drives the engineer to the Flats every morning, and picks him up every evening. They do not converse: "[Frome] seemed a part of the mute melancholy landscape, an incarnation of its frozen woe, with all that was warm and sentient in him fast bound below the surface."

One morning a blizzard hits Starkfield, suspending train service between Corbury Flats and Corbury Junction. Ethan drives the narrator all the way to the Junction, waits for him to finish his business, then begins to drive him home. During the ride back to Starkfield, however, the snowstorm worsens, making the journey nearly impossible. Ethan offers to let the narrator sleep at his farm for the night. The narrator accepts, and follows Ethan into the house, in the silence hearing only "a woman's voice droning querulously." The reader knows that Ethan lives with his wife Zenobia (or Zeena), and therefore assumes that the voice is hers. As the narrator enters the house, he addresses the reader, telling us that "It was that night that I found the clue to Ethan Frome, and began to put together this vision of his story." The Preface ends here with two-and-a-half lines of ellipses, suggesting a significant separation between the Preface and the actual story. The body of the story is written in third-person; the figure of the narrator is completely absent from the story he tells. It is only the Preface and the Epilogue that remind the reader that everything in between is being told by an outsider who did not witness the actual events of the story, and did not even meet Ethan Frome until twenty-four years after his story ends.

Chapter I goes back twenty-four years. Ethan is a young man of twenty-eight years old, and has been married to Zeena for seven years. He walks from his farm into Starkfield in order to meet his wife's cousin, Mattie Silver, at a church dance and walk her home. Mattie has lived with the Fromes for one year, helping about the house because Zeena is sickly (probably a hypochondriac). Mattie is not a native of Starkfield, and Ethan romanticizes her position as an outsider to his world: "[Ethan] had always been more sensitive than the people about him to the appeal of natural beauty . . . But hitherto the emotion had remained in him as a silent ache, veiling with sadness the beauty that evoked it . . . Then he learned that one other spirit had trembled with the same touch of wonder." Ethan's love for Mattie is linked to his desire to escape the stifling closeness and isolation of Starkfield. He sees Mattie dancing with Denis Eady (the same grocer who later drives the narrator to and from Corbury Flats), and becomes jealous of Denis's possible romance with Mattie.

In **Chapter II**, Mattie comes out of the church and Ethan hides in order to observe her interaction with Denis; it is not until she refuses Denis's offer of a ride home that Ethan shows himself to her. They walk home together, arm in arm, and Wharton implies that Mattie returns Ethan's feelings for her. They plan to sled down Corbury Road the next night. When they arrive at the farm, they realize that

Zeena has apparently forgotten to leave the key under the doormat. Zeena waited up for them, presumably because she suspects the potential for an affair between her husband and her cousin. Ethan wants to speak with Mattie alone, but Zeena threateningly convinces him to come upstairs with her.

Chapter III opens the following morning, with Ethan thinking of Mattie and wishing he had kissed her the night before. He remembers how Mattie came to live with them: her parents died when she was twenty years old, and she was left without money or family. She worked for six months as a shopgirl in a department store, but the long hours led to the breakdown of her health. Zeena's doctor suggested that she hire someone to help her with the housework, and the Fromes took in Mattie. The year since Mattie has come to Starkfield has been tense: Ethan loves Mattie, Zeena suspects it, and Zeena therefore does not like Mattie and is rude to her. This morning, Zeena announces that she will spend the night with her aunt in Bettsbridge so she can see a new doctor. Such trips were not without precedent; Ethan usually dreads them because they guarantee the expense of a new doctor and treatment. But today, Ethan is only excited: this will be the first time he and Mattie have been alone together for a night.

In **Chapter IV**, Zeena leaves for Bettsbridge and Ethan goes to town for business. When he returns, the door is locked, but in contrast to the previous night, Mattie opens it warmly. She has prepared a nice dinner, and even took down a special-occasions pickle dish that had been a wedding gift to Zeena. Mattie and Ethan flirt throughout dinner; both behave as though Zeena does not exist, and Mattie is Ethan's wife. During the meal, Zeena's cat jumps onto the table and knocks the pickle dish onto the floor, breaking it into pieces. Ethan places the pieces high on a shelf, hoping to replace it before Zeena notices that it is broken.

Chapter V opens after supper, describing Ethan and Mattie in a warmly domestic scene. They realize that they forgot to go sledding, and Ethan kids Mattie about being frightened of a huge elm tree in the sledding path. She claims not to be afraid of it, but they decide to stay in the house nonetheless. They go to bed separately.

Chapter VI begins the next morning at the breakfast table; Ethan and Mattie are joined by Jotham, Ethan's hired hand around the farm. Ethan hopes to get his work finished early so that he and Mattie can be alone before Zeena returns, but the weather is terrible and the work is slow. Ethan goes into town and buys glue in order to mend the pickle dish, but Zeena has already returned when he arrives home.

In **Chapter VII**, Zeena informs Ethan that the Bettsbridge doctor forbade her to do anything around the house, and that she hired a girl from Bettsbridge to replace Mattie. The new girl is to arrive the next day; Mattie must leave the next day as well. Ethan is furious, and goes down to supper alone. He and Mattie eat in silence, and then he kisses her for the first time, and tells her that she must leave. Zeena comes downstairs complaining of stomach pains; she looks on the highest shelf for stomach powders, and finds the broken pickle dish. She accuses Mattie of purposefully trying to ruin her life, and leaves the room.

Chapter VIII opens in Ethan's study, where he spends the night alone. In the morning, he goes into Starkfield and attempts to borrow fifty dollars so that he and Mattie can flee out west together. On his way, he meets Mrs. Hale (Mrs. Ned Hale's mother), who is kind and is concerned about Zeena's health. Ethan realizes that he is attempting to abandon his sickly wife, and defeated, returns home.

Chapter IX begins later that afternoon. Ethan insists on driving Mattie to the train station. They take the long route to Corbury Flats, and decide to prolong their time together by sledding down the hill. They realize that it is five o'clock and Mattie has missed her train. She suggests that they sled down the hill again, but that this time Ethan aim for the large elm tree so that they can die together and never be parted. Ethan agrees, and they hit the tree, but both survive. The chapter ends with ellipses, signaling the return to the narrator's perspective in the Epilogue.

The Epilogue opens with cessation of the "querulous drone" that ended the Preface. The narrator is in Ethan's kitchen, and he sees two old women sitting around the table. The taller one complains that the other let the fire go down; the roles have reversed, and now Mattie is crippled and cared for by Zeena. As soon as the two women are identified, and the narrator realizes that all three of them— Ethan, Zeena, and Mattie—have lived together in isolation for the past twenty-four years, the narrative skips to the next morning. The narrator does not describe the events or conversation during his night at the Fromes'. Mrs. Hale is amazed that Ethan invited the narrator into his home, saying that he is the first stranger to set foot in the house in over twenty years. She breaks her silence about Ethan and tells the narrator about the sledding "smash-up." When they were found at the bottom of the hill, Mattie was laid in Mrs. Hale's house, and Ethan had been taken to the minister's. Zeena came into town immediately and took them both home with her. The three have lived together at the farm since then, with Zeena caring for Mattie. The text ends with Mrs. Hale saying that she wished Mattie had died: "And I say, if she'd ha' died, Ethan might ha' lived; and the way they are now, I don't see's there's much difference between the Fromes up at the farm and the Fromes down in the graveyard . . ." ❀

List of Characters in
Ethan Frome

The Narrator is not named, but the story is told from his point of view. The prologue and the epilogue are written in the narrator's first-person voice, but the actual story of Ethan, which takes places twenty-four years before the narrator arrives in Starkfield, has been formalized into a third-person narrative (although the "author" is still the narrator).

Ethan Frome, a farmer in Starkfield, is the main character of the novel. The plot centers around his loveless marriage to Zeena, and his forbidden love for her cousin, Mattie Silver.

Zenobia (Zeena) Frome is Ethan's wife. She is sickly (probably a hypochondriac) and jealous of Mattie, with whom she suspects Ethan is in love.

Mattie Silver is Zeena's cousin, who comes to Starkfield to live with the Fromes in order to help Zeena with the housework. She is in love with Ethan, and it is at her suggestion that they attempt to commit a double suicide.

Mrs. Ned Hale (Ruth Varnum), the widow of Ned Hale, boards the narrator during his stay in Starkfield. She was once close friends with Mattie, and the novel closes with her abbreviated and emotional version of Ethan's story.

Denis Eady was one of Mattie's suitors when she first came to Starkfield. Ethan's jealousy of him is the first indication that his love for Mattie exceeds acceptable cousinly limits.

Harmon Gow used to drive the stagecoach between Bettsbridge and Starkfield before the introduction of the train. He is the narrator's first source of information about Ethan.

Jotham Powell is the hired hand on Ethan's farm. He warns Ethan that Zeena is in a "mood" after he picks her up from the train station.
⚙

Critical Views on
Ethan Frome

[Lionel Trilling (1905–1975) was a professor of literature at Columbia University. His works include a collection of essays, *The Liberal Imagination; Sincerity and Authority;* and *The Life and Work of Sigmund Freud.* Here, he discusses the morality, or lack of morality, behind *Ethan Frome.*]

⟨. . .⟩ Her impulse in conceiving the story of Ethan Frome was not, however, that of moral experimentation. It was, as I have said, a purely literary impulse, in the bad sense of the word "literary." Her aim is not that of Wordsworth in any of his stories of the suffering poor, to require of us that we open our minds to a realization of the kinds of people whom suffering touches. Nor is it that of Flaubert in *Madame Bovary,* to wring from solid circumstances all the pity and terror of an ancient tragic fable. Nor is it that of Dickens or Zola, to shake us with the perception of social injustice, to instruct us in the true nature of social life and to dispose us to indignant opinion and action. These are not essentially literary intentions; they are moral intensions. But all that Edith Wharton has in mind is to achieve that grim tableau of which I have spoken, of pain and imprisonment, of life-in-death. About the events that lead up to this tableau, there is nothing she finds to say, nothing whatever. The best we can conclude of the meaning of her story is that it might perhaps be a subject of discourse in the context of rural sociology—it might be understood to exemplify the thesis that love and joy do not flourish on poverty-stricken New England farms. If we try to bring it into the context of morality, its meaning goes no further than certain cultural consider-ations—that is, to people who like their literature to show the "smiling aspects of life," it may be thought to say, "This is the aspect that life really has, as grim as this"; while to people who repudiate a literature that represents only the smiling aspects of life it says, "How intelligent and how brave you are to be able to understand that life is as grim as this." It is really not very much to say.

And yet there is in *Ethan Frome* an idea of considerable impor-tance. It is there by reason of the author's deficiencies, not by reason of her powers—because it suits Edith Wharton's rather dull intention to be content with telling a story about people who do not make moral decisions, whose fate cannot have moral reverberations. The idea is this: that moral inertia, the *not* making of moral decisions, constitutes a large part of the moral life of humanity.

This isn't an idea that literature likes to deal with. Literature is charmed by energy and dislikes inertia. It characteristically represents morality as positive action. The same is true of the moral philosophy of the West—has been true ever since Aristotle defined a truly moral act by its energy of reason, of choice. A later development of this tendency said that an act was really moral only if it went against the inclination of the person performing the act: the idea was parodied as saying that one could not possibly act morally to one's friends, only to one's enemies.

Yet the dull daily world sees something below this delightful preoccupation of literature and moral philosophy. It is aware of the morality of inertia, and of its function as a social base, as a social cement. It knows that duties are done for no other reason than that they are said to be duties; for no other reason, sometimes, than that the doer has not really been able to conceive of any other course—has, perhaps, been afraid to think of any other course. Hobbes said of the Capitol geese that saved Rome by their cackling that they were the salvation of the city, not because they were they but there. How often the moral act is performed not because we are we but because we are there! This is the morality of habit, or the morality of biology. This is Ethan Frome's morality, simple, unquestioning, passive, even masochistic. His duties as a son are discharged because he is a son; his duties as a husband are discharged because he is a husband. He does nothing by moral election. At one point in his story he is brought to moral crisis—he must choose between his habituated duty to his wife and his duty and inclination to the girl he loves. It is quite impossible for him to deal with the dilemma in the high way that literature and moral philosophy prescribe, by reason and choice. Choice is incompatible with his idea of his existence; he can only elect to die.

—Robert MacIver, ed., *Great Moral Dilemmas* (New York: Harper and Bros., 1956).

[Cynthia Griffin Wolff is the Class of 1922 Professor of Literature at the Massachusetts Institute of Technology. In addition to editing the Norton edition of *Ethan Frome,* she published A *Feast of Words: The Triumph of Edith Wharton* and *Emily Dickinson.* Here she discusses the extent to which the narrator's imagination shapes his story.]

⟨. . .⟩ There are literary affinities inherent in the work itself that force themselves upon us. Outside of *Ethan Frome,* for example, there is no other Zenobia in American literature save Hawthorne's heroine in *The Blithedale Romance;* one of the changes that Wharton made from the Black Book *Ethan* was the change of Anna's name to Zeena (Zenobia), though Mattie's name was left unaltered. Hart's name was changed to Ethan. If we wonder why, we might plausibly connect this change with Hawthorne as well, for the only other notable Ethan in American literature is Ethan Brand of Mount Graylock (a geographical neighbor of Wharton's Lenox and psychological kin of the villagers in Starkfield—amongst whom Wharton lived in imagination for ten years). Ethan Brand had found the Unpardonable Sin in a willed isolation from the brotherhood of humanity. Wharton was not interested in sin, but she was interested in the effect of isolation upon the workings of man's emotional life: thus Ethan Frome is related to Ethan Brand; but his deadening isolation is in the cold world of unloved and unloving inner emptiness—a world of depression, loneliness, and slow starvation. Why, in the end, would Wharton be interested in so deliberately suggesting an affinity between her work and the tales of Hawthorne? Again, we must look to the structure of the novel and the role of the narrator for our answer. In much of Hawthorne (and in that most "Hawthornian" of Edith Wharton's stories—"The Eyes"), we follow the tale principally as a revelation of the teller. *The Blithedale Romance* is, ultimately, about Coverdale. Just so, *Ethan Frome* is about its narrator. ⟨. . .⟩

Bearing this fact in mind, let us rush momentarily ahead—to that point in the novel where the "real subject" is generally assumed to begin. An astounding discovery awaits us: the man whom we come to know as the young Ethan Frome is *no more than a figment of the narrator's imagination.* Wharton's method of exposition leaves no doubt. We are not permitted to believe that the narrator is recounting a history of something that actually happened; we are not given leave to speculate that he is passing along a confidence obtained in the dark intimacy of a cold winter's night. No: the "story" of Ethan Frome is introduced in unmistakable terms. "It was that night that I found the clue to Ethan Frome, and began *to put together this vision* of his story . . ." (emphasis mine). Our narrator is a teller of terrible tales, a seer into the realms of dementia. The "story" of Ethan Frome is nothing more than a dream vision, a brief glimpse into the most appalling recesses of the narrator's mind. The overriding question becomes then—not who is Ethan Frome, but who in the world is this ghastly guide to whom we must submit as we read the tale.

The structure demands that we take him into account. Certainly *he* demands it. It is *his* story, ultimately his "vision" of Ethan Frome, that we will get. His vision is as good as any other (so he glibly assures us at the beginning—for "each time it was a different story"), and therefore his story has as much claim to truth as any other. And yet, he is a nervous fellow. The speech pattern is totally unlike Wharton's own narrative style—short sentences, jagged prose rhythms, absolutely no sense of ironic control over the language, no distance from it. Yes, the fellow is nervous. He seems anxious about our reaction and excessively eager to reassure us that had *we* been situated as *he* was, catching a first horrified glimpse of Ethan Frome, we "must have asked who he was." Anyone would. Frome is no mere bit of local color. He is, for reasons that we do not yet understand, a force that compels examination; "the sight pulled me up sharp." (It would pull all of you up sharp, and all of you would have done as I did.)

Certain elements in Wharton's story are to be taken as "real" within the fictional context: Ethan Frome is badly crippled; he sustained his injuries in a sledding accident some twenty-four years ago; he has been in Starkfield for most of his life, excepting a short visit to Florida, living first with his parents and then with his querulous, sickly wife Zeena; there is a third member of the household, his wife's cousin, Miss Mattie Silver; she too was badly crippled in the same sledding accident that felled Ethan. To these facts the various members of the town will all attest—and to *nothing more.* Everything that the reader can accept as reliably true can be found in the narrative frame; everything else bears the imprint of the narrator's

own interpretation—as indeed even the selection of events chroni-
cled in the frame does—and while that interpretation might be as
true as any other, we dare not accept it as having the same validity as
the bare outline presented above. ⟨. . .⟩

> —Cynthia Griffin Wolff, *A Feast of Words: The Triumph of Edith
> Wharton* (New York: Oxford UP, 1977): pp. 163–165.

Elizabeth Ammons on *Ethan Frome* as a Fairy Tale

[Elizabeth Ammons is Professor of English at Tufts University. She is the author of *Edith Wharton's Argument with
America* and *Conflicting Stories: American Women Writers at
the Turn into the Twentieth Century.* Here she discusses the
way *Ethan Frome* can be read as a perverted fairy tale.]

Although finally highly realistic both in its liberal social criticism
and its more sweeping psychological implications, *Ethan Frome* is
designed to read like a fairy tale. It draws on archetypes of the
genre—the witch, the silvery maiden, the honest woodcutter—and
brings them to life in the landscape and social structure of rural New
England. To tell the story Wharton introduces an unnamed, edu-
cated city-dweller, who has had to piece the narrative together; all he
can offer about Ethan, he announces at the end of his preface, is:

> this vision of his story . . . .
> . . . .
> . . . .
> . . . .

Short ellipses often appear in Wharton's fiction, but this ellipsis is
excessive, and it exists to help establish genre. It trails off for three
printed lines to emphasize that, while Ethan's story will appear real
and we can believe that the tragedy did happen, the version here is a
fabrication. It is an imagined reconstruction of events organized in
part out of shared oral material and shaped for us into one of many
possible narratives. As the narrator says in his opening statement: "I
had the story bit by bit, from various people, and, as generally hap-

pens in such cases, each time it was a different story." This tale, in other words, belongs to a community of people (ourselves now included) and has many variants. Also important is Wharton's selection of the word "vision." Not a documentary term, "vision" prepares us for the fact that Ethan's story, with its vivid use of inherited symbols and character types, will seem a romance or fairy tale. ⟨. . .⟩

Specifically, a network of imagery and event in *Ethan Frome* calls up the fairy tale *Snow-White*. The frozen landscape, the emphasis on sevens, the physical appearance of Mattie Silver (black hair, red cheeks, white skin), her persecution by witchlike Zeena (an older woman who takes the girl in when her mother dies and thus serves as a stepmother to her), Mattie's role as housekeeper: all have obvious parallels in the traditional fairy tale about a little girl whose jealous stepmother tries to keep her from maturing into a healthy, marriageable young woman. Although Wharton is not imitating this well-known fairy tale—rather, she draws on familiar elements of *Snow-White* as touchstones for a new, original fairy tale—still, for many readers, without their even realizing it, the implicit contrast between Zeena's victory in *Ethan Frome* and the stepmother's defeat in *Snow-White* no doubt contributes to the terror of Wharton's story. Most fairy tales reassure by teaching that witches lose in the end. Children and heroines (Snow-Whites) do not remain the victims of ogres. Someone saves them. Here is part of the horror of *Ethan Frome*: Wharton's modern fairy tale for adults, while true to traditional models in the way it teaches a moral about "real" life at the same time that it addresses elemental fears (e.g., the fear of death, the fear of being abandoned), does not conform to the genre's typical denouement. The lovers do not live happily ever after. The witch wins.

Zeena's face alone would type her as a witch. Sallow-complexioned and old at thirty-five, her bloodless countenance is composed of high protruding cheekbones, lashless lids over piercing eyes, thin colorless hair, and a mesh of minute vertical lines between her gaunt nose and granite chin. Black calico, with a brown shawl in winter, makes up her ordinary daytime wear, and her muffled body is as fleshless as her face. Late one night Ethan and Mattie return from a church dance to the dreary house where a "dead cucumber-vine dangled from the porch like the crape streamer tied to the door for a death." They are met by Zeena: "Against the dark background of the kitchen she stood up tall and angular, one hand drawing a quilted counterpane to her flat breast, while the other held a lamp. The light, on a level with her chin, drew out of the darkness her puckered throat and the projecting wrist of the hand that clutched the quilt, and deepened fantastically the hollows and prominences of her high-boned face." Confronting the youthful couple at midnight in her kitchen, "which had the deadly chill of a vault," Ethan's spectral wife, complete with stealthy, destructive cat, appears the perfect witch of nursery lore.

Mattie Silver, in contrast, seems a fairy maiden, a princess of nature in Ethan's eyes. Her expressive face changes "like a wheat-field under a summer breeze," and her voice reminds him of "a rustling covert leading to enchanted glades." When she sews, her hands flutter like birds building a nest; when she cries, her eyelashes feel like butterflies. Especially intoxicating is her luxuriant dark hair, which curls like the tendrils on a wildflower and is "soft yet springy, like certain mosses on warm slopes." By candlelight her hair looks "like a drift of mist on the moon." Simone de Beauvoir, quoting Michel Carrouges, provides in general terms a nearly perfect description of Mattie's psychomythic significance for Ethan: "Woman is not the useless replica of man, but rather the enchanted place where the living alliance between man and nature is brought about. If she should disappear, men would be alone, strangers lacking passports in an icy world. She is the earth itself raised to life's summit, the earth become sensitive and joyous; and without her, for man the earth is mute and dead." Zeena's colors are those of the dead earth—black, grey, brown; Mattie's are blood red and snowy white. She sleeps under a red and white quilt, wears a crimson ribbon and a cherry red "fascinator," and has rosy lips and a quick blush. A vision of her face lingers with Ethan one morning: "It was part of the sun's red and of the pure glitter on the snow." Passion and purity mingle in Ethan's image of Mattie, making her more valuable to him (but no more attainable) than the precious metal her last name specifies.

—Elizabeth Ammons, Edith Wharton's Argument with America
(Athens: University of Georgia Press, 1980): pp. 61–64.

[Candace Waid is Associate Professor of English at the University of California at Santa Barbara. She has published *Edith Wharton's Letters from the Underworld: Fictions of Women and Writing,* and edited the Norton edition of *The Age of Innocence.* Here she discusses ways in which the story is based upon infertility.]

The vision of *Ethan Frome* is finally a vision of unrelenting infertility. The suicide attempt that cripples Mattie and Ethan is prefigured in the smashed pickle dish, "the bits of broken glass" that Zeena discovers and holds "as if she carried a dead body . . ." (Wharton's ellipses). The shattered pickle dish that is Zeena's most treasured wedding gift and the dead cucumber vine that makes Frome imagine Zeena's death are emblems of a lost or past fertility. The smashed glass under the foot of the bridegroom should symbolize the loss of virginity and the beginning of fertility; but the pickle dish, used or unused, can symbolize infertility only. The dead cucumber vine that "dangled from the porch like a crape streamer tied to the door for a death" suggests the past fertility of an umbilical cord that now marks the barren interior of a house deprived of its "actual hearth-stone." One critic has remarked that a "cucumber is no more than a pickle," yet without entering the ongoing critical debate about the vegetable symbols in the novel, it is essential to acknowledge that a pickle is a preserve that cannot reproduce itself. In the magical supper that Frome and Mattie have during their evening alone, the pickle dish and pickles form a display, a kind of rehearsal, for the eroticized scene of the accident that finally breaks the vessel of the young woman's body and preserves her in infertility. Both the broken pickle dish and the breaking of the body of the young woman suggest the horror of fertility rituals gone awry.

In the narrator's vision, the fragments of the dish and Mattie Silver's body cannot be put back together again. Only the narrator's story projected onto the shards of the past (which he claims to have gathered "bit by bit") can form the mocking semblance of a whole and seamless narrative. The narrative also has an ominous inevitability and circularity. *Ethan Frome* has its beginning in its ending: at the beginning of the story the narrator describes the crippled Frome, whose face "looks as if he was dead and in hell now!" The vision of the narrator must end in this hell because the future of the story he tells will always be in the past. In the introduction Wharton remarks that her "tale was not one on which many variations could be played." The narrator's vision may contain variations, but the story must end in the same place, around the same barren hearth. ⟨. . .⟩

The narrator, who has imagined that Frome took "a year's course at a technological college at Worcester, and dabbled in the laboratory with a friendly professor of physics," pictures him in his "cold dark 'study'" with his books and "an engraving of Abraham Lincoln and a calendar with 'Thoughts from the Poets'." Earlier in the empty kitchen Frome has found "a scrap of paper torn from the back of a seedsman's catalogue, on which three words were written: 'Don't trouble, Ethan.'" He reads "the message again and again." Although at first "the possession of the paper gave him a strange new sense of her nearness," he realizes that "henceforth they would have no other way of communicating with each other" besides "cold paper and dead words!" (Later when Mattie says, "You must write to me sometimes," he responds, "Oh, what good'll writing do?") He starts to write a letter to his wife telling her that he has run off with Mattie, but after reading "the seductive words" of an advertisement for trips to the West, he has second thoughts: "The paper fell from his hand and he pushed aside his unfinished letter."

Like Lily Bart, Frome tries to imagine an alternate plot for his unbearable story, but leaving his letter unfinished, he resigns himself to being a prisoner for life. Moments before Ethan and Mattie decide to attempt suicide, Mattie produces the unfinished letter: "She tore the letter in shreds and sent them fluttering off into the snow." Soon her "words" of desperation are "like fragments torn from his heart," and the failed suicide attempt leaves both of them torn and shattered. Mattie's elliptical message written on "the seeds-man's catalogue" emphasizes Ethan's failure as a seedman. Later he strokes her hair so that the feeling of it "would sleep there like a seed in winter," but these winter seeds bear no fruit. Like the woman whose "page" is torn by Vesalius, her life will be "ripened" only to a "bud of death"— in the words of Wharton's Margaret of Cortona, a "lifeless blossom in the Book of Life." Writing under the calendar with 'Thoughts from the Poets,' Frome sees only "cold paper and dead words." Here the seeds of writing, despite the possibility of "seductive words," are not the seeds of the pomegranate—either the maternal fertility of Demeter or the transgressive eroticism of Persephone. The words on the seed catalogue cannot even lead to an alternate underworld of death. The cost of vision in this story is a failure of mortality as well as immortality as the characters are left imprisoned in a living death. The "symbol of a man, / The sign-board creaking o'er an empty inn," that pictures the barrenness of both women and rockbound New England in the novel is also a sign for the failure of words to generate life.

—Candace Waid, *Edith Wharton's Letters from the Underworld: Fictions of Women and Writing* (Chapel Hill: The University of North Carolina Press, 1991): pp. 75–78.

Mary D. Lagerwey-Voorman and Gerald E. Markle on Edith Wharton's Sick Role

[Mary D. Lagerwey-Voorman is an Assistant Professor in the school of nursing at Western Michigan University. In 1998 she published her book *Reading Auschwitz*. Gerald E. Markle is Professor of Sociology at Western Michigan University. He has published several books, including *Minutes to Midnight: Nuclear Weapons Protest in America*. Here they examine the ways in which Ethan, Zeena, and Mattie fulfill (or deny) the social "sick role."]

From the narrator's perspective, Ethan's quest to fulfill dreams and values is in conflict with his socially circumscribed position in rural New England. He has dreamed of an education, of moving away, and of living with a woman with whom he experiences mutual attraction. But he is unsuccessful in his attempts to re-negotiate the obligations placed on him by the sick roles of a succession of family members: his father, his mother, and now Zeena. ⟨...⟩

In contrast to Zeena, Mattie and Ethan are not entitled to the exemptions and obligations of the sick role. Mattie was too ill for stenography, book-keeping, or department store clerking prior to joining the Fromes. Yet, as a domestic servant, her health and illness are irrelevant to Zeena. It does nor entitle her to medical care not rest:

> The pure air, and the long summer hours in the open, gave back life and elasticity to Mattie, and Zeena, with more leisure to devote to her complex ailments, grew less watchful of the girl's omissions.

Ethan and Zeena disagree on Mattie's household status:

> "Mattie Silver's not a hired girl. She's your relation."
> "She's a pauper that's hung unto us all after her father's done his best to ruin us. I've kep' her here a whole year: it's somebody else's turn now."

Zeena's sick role gives her some control over Ethan, but is ineffective in allowing her to claim a middle or upper-class identity. Her sick role gives Ethan sympathy in the community, but does not add to his status. In middle and upper-classes, a wife's idleness, delicacy, and the leisure to take on a sick role proved her husband's success (Ehrenreich and English). By contrast, Ethan tries to convince Zeena that she is "a poor man's wife . . . but I'll do the best I can for you." She is not able to claim all of the secondary gains of the sick role because of the working-class status of her husband. Her anger at Ethan for not supporting her in her sick role reflects a broader but ineffective protest against the Frome's economic status. "Better send me over to the almshouse and be done with it . . . I guess there's been Fromes there afore now."

From the narrator's perspective, Ethan has sustained a major injury. Ethan was "the ruin of a man." "The look in his face . . . neither poverty nor physical suffering could have put it there." Yet Ethan is never allowed to take on the sick role. Instead, he is locked into a care-giver role. ⟨. . .⟩

The sick role may define the identity of both those who are ill and those in reciprocal roles. Mattie and Ethan stand as role partners who support Zeena's sick role. Purportedly, Ethan had given up an education to care for his parents. He has cared for Zeena for six years, and imagines a future with Mattie in which he would take care of her when she is sick. "I want to do for you and care for you. I want to be there when you're sick and when you're lonesome."

Ethan's financial obligations are considerable, and do not abate even as he questions the efficacy of treatment:

> Her husband had grown to dread these expeditions because of their cost. Zeena always came back laden with expensive remedies, and her last visit to Springfield had been commemorated by her paying twenty dollars for an electric battery of which she had never been able to learn the use.

Ethan's attempts to negotiate the norms of the sick role to his advantage are met with failure. He briefly contemplates using the financial burden of Zeena's illness to gain an advance payment from the mill for:

> suddenly it occurred to him that Andrew Hale, who was a kind-hearted man, might be induced to reconsider his refusal and advance a small sum on the lumber if he were told that Zeena's ill-health made it necessary to hire a ser-vant . . . and with fifty dollars in his pocket nothing could keep him from Mattie.

He is met, instead, by the builder's wife, who effectively blocks this avenue of escape with her pity: "I don't know anybody round here's had more sickness than Zeena . . . I always tell Mr. Hale I don't know what she'd 'a' done if she hadn't 'a' had you to look after her. You've had an awful mean time, Ethan Frome." He loses courage when Mrs. Hale legitimizes Zeena's illness, offers him sympathy, and reminds him of his responsibilities to Zeena. Her sympathy underscores the binding responsibilities Zeena's illness have placed on him, and places those obligations in a community context. For both Zeena and Ethan, economic and community forces determine their options in relationship to the sick role.

—Mary D. Lagerwey-Voorman and Gerald E. Markle, "Edith Wharton's Sick Role," *The Sociological Quarterly* 35, no. 1 (1994): pp. 123–125.

[Kathy A. Fedorko teaches at Middlesex County College. She has published *Gender and the Gothic in the Fiction of Edith Wharton,* from which this excerpt is taken. Here she discusses the extent to which Ethan, Zeena, and Mattie can be seen as different aspects of the same personality.]

Through her narrator's immersion in his/Ethan's psyche that entering the cold house enacts, Wharton encourages us to see Ethan, Zeena, and Mattie Silver as elements of a single self, projections of the narrator's fears about femininity and masculinity. She does this also by referring to them all as "*my granite outcroppings; but half-emerged from the soil, and scarcely more articulate*" and by drawing crucial parallels among them in their portrayal. Each is defined in good part through nature images. Mattie is the most definitively "natural": the motion of her mind was "as incalculable as the flit of a bird in the branches" and her hands are compared to a pair of birds; her lashes are like "netted butterflies"; she droops before Ethan like "a broken branch"; "the call of a bird in a mountain ash was so like her laughter"; her hair is "like certain mosses on warm slopes" and "smelt of the woods." After the crash Ethan mistakes her for "a little animal twittering."

Zeena is less appealingly but no less naturally portrayed as "a shape of stone" wearing "a stony image of resentment" and bearing "hollows and prominences" on her high-boned face. During Ethan and Mattie's tête-à-tête over dinner Zeena is personified by her cat, jumping between the two onto Zeena's chair at the table and later onto her rocker and breaking the incriminating pickle dish. Ethan, with his "great height," his "powerful look," his stiffness, his lean brown head, and his "brown seamed profile," is an image of the trees he cuts down, makes into lumber, and hauls into town. The narrator's first impression of him is that "he seemed a part of the mute melancholy landscape." All three characters are only slightly more articulate than the bird, moss, cat, and trees to which they are compared.

More striking and significant are the passivity and paralysis of spirit they share, their inability to live lives of fulfilled love, and the allure they each find in death. Mattie, like Lily Bart, is an orphan with no particular life skills who has apparently played no role in determining her own future. Though attracted to Ethan, she has no plan to act on her attraction other than to suggest that they commit suicide together. Her eventual physical paralysis figures her internal passivity.

Ethan has had the eagerness to travel and live in towns "where there were lectures and big libraries and 'fellows doing things,'" but he marries a woman who serves as a mother substitute and submits to her preference for stasis. Having chosen a mate out of neediness rather than love, he is paralyzed by guilt when he tries to extricate himself and attempts suicide rather than acting on his desire for Mattie. A "despairing sense of his helplessness" seizes him when faced with his wife's intent to send Mattie away. That he chooses death as an expression of desire is prefigured by the "warm sense of continuance and stability" the family graveyard gives him and by his dream of lying in it next to Mattie.

Zeena's absorption in her ailments, whether real or imagined, is her chosen form of physical gratification. Unhappy with her life and strong willed, she has nevertheless done nothing about her unhappiness other than dwell on it and her ever-impending death. With her "drawn and bloodless face" she is a living ghost, a spectral presence in the kitchen, which has "the deadly chill of a vault." Probably little loved herself, she is now as an adult incapable of showing or receiving love. As she says reflectively of her geraniums and no doubt of herself, "they pine away when they ain't cared for."

Another element encouraging us to see Ethan Frome, Zeena Frome, and Mattie Silver as elements of a single self is their alternating roles as caretakers and the one taken care of. Ethan cares for his parents and then is cared for by Zeena, who helps him tend to his mother. Zeena becomes the one in need of care until Mattie is disabled, at which point Zeena becomes the one who tends to her. Mattie is unwanted until she is taken in by Ethan and Zeena. She tends to their needs until she becomes like Zeena—gray haired, bloodless of face, and helpless. "I guess it's always Ethan done the caring," Harmon Gow says of him, but as the narrator comments, "there were perceptible gaps between his facts."

Ethan and Zeena also alternately exchange dominance in their relationship with one another. Zeena's "hard perpendicular bonnet" and Ethan's "helmet like-peak" on his cap suggest their common strength, to the point of rigidity. Ethan wields power by not listening to Zeena, while she wields it with her silence. Like the Duke in the earlier story "The Duchess at Prayer" and like the Duke de Ercole in the later story "Kerfol," Zeena's "fault-finding was of the silent kind, but not the less penetrating for that." She has the same stealthy, suspicious alertness to her husband's habits that both men in the short stories have to their wives' ways.

Despite his potential strength, Ethan is rendered immobile by the dread common to those who face primal emotions characteristic of the Gothic experience. Since the previous night when Zeena had come to the door to let Ethan and Mattie in after their intimate walk home, "a vague dread had hung on his sky-line." Then "his dread was so strong that, man-like, he sought to postpone certainty," reminding us that in Wharton's Gothic it is usually men who resist confronting their fear. Yet both Zeena and Ethan end up with the halting gait of broken spirits; she has a "dragging down-at-the-heel step," while he drags himself across the brick pavement, with a "lameness checking each step like the jerk of a chain." Though it is Ethan who feels himself "a prisoner for life," Zeena, and eventually Mattie as well, are no less imprisoned in their lives. Masculinity and femininity blend and waver in the narrator's vision, a horrifying yet potentially restorative insight into his worst fear, of inarticulate, immobile, impotent existence. His courage in plunging imaginatively into the abyss prepares the way for characters in Wharton's subsequent Gothic fiction to claim their eroticism and their will.

—Kathy A. Fedorko, *Gender and the Gothic in the Fiction of Edith Wharton* (Tuscaloosa: University of Alabama Press, 1995): pp. 63–65.

Plot Summary of
The Custom of the Country

Book I of *The Custom of the Country* begins in the Hotel Stentorian in New York City. Undine Spragg, who has been living there with her parents for two years, receives an invitation to a dinner given by Laura Fairford, the sister of Ralph Marvell, whom Undine met the previous evening at a party. The Spraggs moved to New York from Apex City, Kansas, hoping that Undine would meet and marry a wealthy society man. The move has been so far unsuccessful, lending importance to the Fairford dinner invitation.

Undine finds the dinner boring, and feels patronized because her lack of knowledge prevents her from participating in the conversation about art and literature. The next day, Undine visits an art gallery in order to educate herself; she sees Peter van Degen, one of the wealthiest men in New York. At the opera a few nights later, she is visited by Popple, the society painter; he introduces her to Peter van Degen (who remembers her from the art gallery). Later, Ralph visits her, and the chapter closes with Ralph's thoughts about the invasion of "new" society (e.g., the van Degens) into "old" society (e.g., the Dagonets and Marvells). Ralph is of course a member of "old" society, and sees the rise of "new" money as a type of violent invasion of an aboriginal society.

Ralph and Undine become engaged, and one night at the opera, Undine sees Elmer Moffatt, also an immigrant from Apex. Wharton hints at some sort of previous (and disgraceful) relationship between them. Undine is frightened that Moffatt's appearance in New York will ruin her upcoming marriage to Ralph; he promises not to reveal their past acquaintance if Undine introduces him to the influential members of Ralph's set. She agrees, does not tell Ralph about her meeting with Elmer, and urges him to push forward the date of the marriage.

Book II opens in Siena, Italy, where Undine and Ralph Marvell are honeymooning. Four months since their marriage, tensions remain below the surface, but it is apparent that the marriage is doomed. Ralph and Undine have completely different ideas of how they would like to live. For instance, in Siena, Ralph is perfectly happy with the silence and nature, while Undine is bored. Although the couple is low in money, she begs Ralph to take her to a more social center in Europe. One month later they are established in St. Moritz, and a loan from Ralph's sister allows them to continue to Paris. Undine sees Peter van Degen in Paris, and complains about Ralph's "tightfistedness." Peter offers her a ride back to New York on his private yacht, and she accepts. Ralph, however, is appalled; he explains that Peter's set is not respectable in the eyes of "old" New York, and that it would disgrace him and his family if she socialized with him. She concedes only if she can stay in Paris until October. Several months later, Undine tells Ralph that she is pregnant; he is thrilled, but she resents the child that will interrupt her life for a full year.

The novel skips forward, and we next see Undine three years later at a tea given by Popple, celebrating the unveiling of his portrait of her. It is her son, Paul's, birthday, and Undine misses his party because she takes a carriage ride with Peter after the tea. Undine explains to Ralph that the portrait sitting went longer than expected; he does not believe her, but accepts the explanation. He finally "gives up" on Undine, recognizing that he loved an imagined personality, not Undine. He finally sees Undine clearly, and understands that "they were fellow-victims in the *noyade* of marriage, but if they ceased to struggle perhaps the drowning would be easier for both . . ."

Paul has been ill, adding to the Marvells' expenses. Undine sees Moffatt, and he asks her to introduce him to Ralph, offering to involve Ralph in a potentially profitable business deal in return for social contacts. The deal is successful, and Undine plans a trip to Europe; Ralph stays in New York. Undine suggests to Peter that they divorce their spouses and marry each other (Peter is married to Ralph's cousin Clare), but Peter refuses. Undine is introduced to Comte Raymond de Chelles, and flirts with him in order to make Peter jealous. She finally threatens to marry Raymond, and Peter promises he will do anything to keep her, even divorce his wife.

Book III describes Ralph's solitary life in New York. He works constantly in order to support Undine's lifestyle, and spends his free time with Paul. Undine rarely answers his regular letters. Ralph becomes seriously ill, and Laura wires Undine, asking her to come home. Undine ignores the telegram and travels to Italy with Peter. While Ralph is recovering, he learns that Undine has filed for divorce. In the very public case, Ralph is portrayed as a greedy husband too absorbed in business to pay attention to his wife. His case is used by society as an example of the growing obsession with wealth; ironically, this is indeed what motivated the divorce, but the obsession is not Ralph's, but Undine's.

Wharton skips ahead one year. Undine succeeded in divorcing Ralph. She left Peter in Europe and traveled to Dakota to get her divorce; Peter had planned to meet her there, but he never arrived. Undine later learns that Peter abandoned her because he was appalled that she refused to care for Ralph while he was ill. Now a divorcee, Undine returns to New York and is shunned by her old friends. Selling a pearl necklace given to her by Peter, Undine finances a trip to Europe for herself and her parents. Mr. and Mrs. Spragg stay in Europe only a short time, leaving Undine in Paris. Even in France she feels excluded from her old social circle. In December, she travels to the Riviera at the suggestion of a doctor, where she becomes friends with Princess Estradina, Raymond de Chelles' cousin. The Princess reintroduces Undine to Raymond while on a visit to Nice.

By the spring, Raymond is in love with Undine. He suggests that she have her marriage annulled (his Catholic family does not recognize divorce), but Undine cannot afford the cost. She asks Moffatt for the money, and he suggests that Undine send for her son, who is legally in her custody. Ralph is very fond of Paul, and Moffatt correctly imagines that he would pay Undine in order to keep Paul in New York. Ralph refuses to send the six-year-old to Undine. He borrows money from his family and invests in a promising business deal, hoping to profit enough to "pay off" Undine. The deal fails, and Ralph is forced to send Paul to Undine. He visits Moffatt, who confesses that he was married to Undine nine years earlier, in Opake, Nebraska. Her parents disapproved of the marriage, and succeeded in negotiating a divorce. Moffatt represents the group of new businessmen that Ralph sees as invading "old" society. Shocked that his ex-wife was once married to such a vulgar man, Ralph goes home, and commits suicide by shooting himself in the head.

Book IV begins after Undine's marriage to Raymond. Paul lives with her in Paris, and she receives an allowance for him from the Dagonets. Raymond suggests that he and Undine leave Paris and move to his ancestral estate in the country, St-Désert. They spend the summer there, and Undine is unhappy being so far away from the social activity of Paris (recall her similar dissatisfaction in Italy during her honeymoon with Ralph). Raymond becomes bored with Undine, traveling a lot and presumably having affairs with other women. Undine is furious when Raymond tells her that she cannot go to Paris that spring because of financial difficulties. She suggests that they sell St-Désert; Raymond is appalled at the suggestion. Like Ralph, Raymond prioritizes tradition and family over money and luxury. Undine still does not understand this mentality, and she invites an appraiser from Paris to examine the famous de Chelles tapestries. Moffatt, now enormously wealthy, is the potential buyer, and accompanies the appraiser to St-Désert. Raymond discovers Undine's attempt to sell the tapestries, and is furious; the two become essentially estranged.

Undine remains in Paris, and becomes close to Moffatt. She suggests that they have an affair. Moffatt refuses, saying that he wants to marry her. He asks her to return to New York with him, where he will help her get a divorce.

Two years later, Undine is married to Moffatt, and they live in an enormous house in Paris. They were able to buy the de Chelles tapestries, which now hang in their home. Paul is nine years old, and he comes home from school to find that both of his "parents" (Undine and Moffatt) are out. They are preparing to throw a large dinner party that night, and don't have very much time to welcome Paul home. Undine suggests that Moffatt become an ambassador, and is upset when he tells her that she could never be an ambassador's wife because she is divorced. The novel ends with Undine's discontentment: "She had learned that there was something she could never get, something that neither beauty nor influence nor millions could ever buy for her. She could never be an Ambassador's wife; and as she advanced to welcome her first guests she said to herself that it was the one part she was really made for." ✿

List of Characters in
The Custom of the Country

Undine Spragg is the main character. She is a social climber from Apex City, Kansas, and comes to New York City in order to establish herself in society through marriage and wealth. The plot revolves around her gradual ascent in New York society through successive marriages and divorces.

Ralph Marvell, the first man Undine marries in the novel, is a member of "old" New York society. He has an impeccable lineage, but not as much money as some members of "new" society (e.g., the van Degens). His genuine and idealistic love for Undine leads him to despair when she divorces him and takes custody of their son; his suicide symbolizes the impossibility of "old" society surviving in "new" New York.

Abner E. and **Leota B. Spragg** are Undine's parents. They are unconcerned with their own social standing, but spend most of their money helping satisfy Undine's demands.

Elmer Moffatt is also from Apex City, and was secretly married to (and divorced from) Undine when they were teenagers. He appears in New York at the same time as Undine, and threatens to reveal their marriage to the Marvells unless Undine and her father help provide him with business "tips" and contacts. His business-made wealth, and his brash and ambitious attitude, mark him as the antithesis of Ralph and "old" society; his ultimate reconciliation with Undine identifies her as the female counterpart to the new, rich, businessman.

Peter van Degen, Ralph's cousin-in-law, has an affair with Undine. His promise to divorce his wife and marry Undine prompts her to divorce Ralph. He ultimately refuses to marry her, ironically because he is appalled at her cruel attitude toward Ralph.

Clare van Degen is Ralph's cousin, and is married to Peter van Degen. She and Ralph were sweethearts when they were younger, and are presumably still in love with each other. She provides a contrast to Undine, and seems to be the "correct" wife for Ralph.

Paul Marvell is the son of Ralph and Undine. After her divorce from Ralph, Undine gains custody of Paul in order to receive more money from Ralph (she needs money so she can have her marriage annulled and thus marry Raymond). This loss of his son compels Ralph to commit suicide.

Comte Raymond de Chelles is a member of the French nobility. Undine flirts with him in order to make Peter van Degen jealous. After Undine's divorce from Ralph, he marries her. Like Ralph, Raymond is no longer enormously wealthy, and Undine is unhappy with their secluded life in the country. With Moffatt's help, Undine divorces him.

Mrs. Heeny is the Spraggs' (and others') manicurist; she is appreciated for her knowledge of the latest gossip and her collection of newspaper clippings from the Society section. She is one of the few characters who appears throughout the story.

Charles Bowen, like Mrs. Heeny, reappears throughout the novel. He functions as a sort of anthropologist interpreting Undine's progress. He argues that the problem with American marriages is that the husbands do not have enough respect for their wives.

Laura Fairford is Ralph Marvell's sister. She is representative of the "old" New York society that ultimately disappoints Undine in its lack of flash and glamour.

Claud Walsingham Popple is a painter known for his portraits of society ladies. Upon her arrival in New York, Undine thinks he is a member of high society; she is quickly corrected by Ralph. Popple paints a beautiful portrait of Undine while she is married to Ralph.

Indiana Frusk is Undine's childhood rival from Apex City who married Undine's first suitor, Millard Binch. Undine views her as a warning about what she could have become had she stayed in Apex. In Paris, Undine learns that Indiana divorced Binch and married the wealthy and influential James J. Rolliver.

Princess Estradina (**Lili**), Raymond's cousin, meets Undine in the Riviera. She reintroduces Undine to Raymond, thinking they will have an affair. ❀

Critical Views on
The Custom of the Country

[Gary H. Lindberg (1941–86) was a Professor of English at
the University of New Hampshire, which established the
annual Lindberg Award in 1986. He published *The Confidence Man in American Literature* and *Edith Wharton and
the Novel of Manners.* Here he discusses the way in which
Wharton, through the figure of Undine, manipulates the
genre of the "novel of manners."]

It is, however, not only the assumptions about the operative social
orders that blunt the force of narrative crises here, but Undine's own
nature as well. There is nothing in Undine corresponding to the
cleavage between Lily's social ambitions and her deeper impulses
and repugnances; all of Undine's yearnings align her with a public
existence as all of her perceptions are shared by a social class. Thus
neither of the antagonisms that sharpen the issues of Lily's story—
that between the social order and the public self or that between the
public and the buried selves—appears in Undine's story. Again, this
phenomenon could be attributed to the kind of story being told, but
not entirely. It is easier to dramatize the widening cleavage between
self and society in a story of social decline than in a story of accruing
success, and as the protagonist more readily questions his ties to an
inimical than to a sustaining reality, the story of social decline can
readily dramatize a splitting of the self as well. But novels of manners have often dealt with ascent through the classes, and a conventional mode of irony has been developed within the genre to
preserve the distance between individual and class. As one sees in
such stories as those of Julien Sorel, Eugène de Rastignac, and Silas
Lapham, the social ascent characteristically entails a moral deterioration, which often becomes perceptible, at least in the end, to the protagonist himself. This mode of irony does not operate in *The Custom
of the Country* because movement through the classes does not
change Undine in any serious way. Although Wharton emphasizes
another kind of irony in showing Undine's success to be perfectly
empty, it is clear that social triumph costs Undine nothing, morally

or personally. She may gain power to effect her will, thus looming larger as a threat, but Undine's moral predisposition is no worse at the end than at the beginning, and her estimate of herself remains impervious to experience.

Clearly, then, the materials of the overt plot in *The Custom of the Country* are intractable, at least within the framework of Wharton's concerns for public and personal issues. It is, of course, possible to dismiss the book as mere social satire and Undine as pure caricature—in other words, to see Wharton as simply releasing her irritation with the "invaders" of old New York. But such a reading accounts for neither the power of the novel, the disturbing force of Undine as a character, nor the perplexing relationship of author and heroine. And it ignores the predispositions of Edith Wharton's art. This is an art of discrimination and disjunction; it exploits observable conflicts in behavior, value, and intention. She gets hold of her stories by locating those social and personal issues that can produce dramatic encounters, outward resistances, and morally significant crises. These habits pertain not only to her ways of telling stories but to her ways of thinking and analyzing as well. And the expectations fostered by these habits govern one's experience of *The Custom of the Country.* That is, this novel not only does not show outward conflict over comprehensible issues but makes it painfully clear that conflict is being dissolved, that potentially dramatic issues are being blurred. Similarly, Wharton not only shows little of importance happening within Undine herself but makes it portentous and disquieting that so little happens. It is the buried fable that puts such expectations into this novel, creates its strange power, and makes one question what it is really about. For while one follows what is happening, one is forced to recognize what is *not* happening.

—Gary H. Lindberg, *Edith Wharton and the Novel of Manners* (Charlottesville: UP Virginia, 1975): pp. 70–71.

[Cynthia Griffin Wolff is the Class of 1922 Professor of Literature at the Massachusetts Institute of Technology. In addition to editing the Norton edition of *Ethan Frome,* she published *A Feast of Words: The Triumph of Edith Wharton,* and *Emily Dickinson.* Here she analyzes the character of Ralph Marvell.]

Even the most important transaction in Ralph's life is contaminated by this deadly lassitude. The details of the separation, where the interests of his son most intimately concern him, slip unnoticed through his limp figures. He receives his wife's legal application for divorce and locks "it away in his desk without mentioning the matter to any one. He supposed that with the putting away of this document he was thrusting the whole subject out of sight." Indeed, he is so eager not to be worried by the matter that he declines even to read it or to examine the terms that he has tacitly accepted. Much later, he realizes that his inaction has given Undine full custody of their son "and he, Ralph Marvell, a sane man, young, able-bodied, in full possession of his wits, had assisted at the perpetration of this abominable wrong, has passively forfeited his right to the flesh of his body, the blood of his being." The son of the vanquished has been lost into captivity, and the last act of Ralph's tragedy has begun. Is Undine a despoiler? Perhaps. But perhaps the seeds of defeat have grown inexorably out of the same soil that bore the last generation of a loftier race.

Wharton wrote no more devastating comment on the world of her childhood and youth than this. Even here, however, her criticism is neither wholesale nor random. Like a surgeon who seeks to preserve by removing only diseased organs, Wharton focuses her satirical thrust with agonizing sharpness. Much in old New York has value. Two elements within it threaten to destroy all the rest; and from these two deadly faults, all other evils follow.

The first is the tendency to withdraw from the rest of society and to ignore everything that is difficult or "common" or "not nice": the adoption of a determinedly unrealistic attitude. In this novel, there are any number of casual allusions to the feminine token that has so often served as Wharton's emblem of this inclination—for instance, the "black cashmere and *two veils*" that Mrs. Marvell wears when she goes to see her ostracized divorced friend (old New York's general squeamishness on the subject of divorce was very much in Wharton's mind just now, and the Aborigines' sense of scandal at it appears more than once in this novel). However, in *The Custom of the Country,* the principal, vast, grotesque representation of retreat is Ralph's secret world, his cavernous, sounding kingdom beneath the sea—weaving a "secret curtain about him"—eventually annihilating him in the isolated splendor of his broken dreams.

The second focus of Wharton's rage is the denial of normal, natural life energy. She draws for us a society where vitality has failed, a world that stifles initiative in children and encourages haphazard dilettantism in adults. The possession of energy and initiative is not sufficient to prove the merit of a social system. However, it is a necessary condition for any society's survival. Without it, all else—however valuable—will inevitably perish.

Ralph takes a rather fatalistic view of his accumulated failures. He concludes wearily "that the weakness was innate in him. He had been eloquent enough, in his free youth, against the conventions of his class; yet when the moment came to show his contempt for them they had mysteriously mastered him, deflecting his course like some hidden hereditary failing." It is typical of Ralph that he should construe his situation thus, for it removes from him the onus of striving to change. There is a large measure of truth in his conclusion, for the options offered by old New York are limiting indeed. Yet it is equally true that for whatever reason, Ralph has built his life around the most pernicious of those options. He has spent all his emotion in passive fantasy instead of manifesting the kind of genuine commitment of family that is intrinsic in his sister's sensitive and tender ministrations. He has allowed his powers of observation and judgment entirely to atrophy so that he has neither the rudimentary cunning of his grandfather nor the sensible analytic capacities of Mr. Bowen. Free and at the same time inevitably shaped by the conditions that particularize his life, Ralph is a haunting specter of the terrible possibilities that are latent in his venerable world.

—Cynthia Griffin Wolff, *A Feast of Words: The Triumph of Edith Wharton* (New York: Oxford UP, 1977): pp. 239–240.

[Wayne W. Westbrook has published articles on Whitman and Dickens; and a book entitled *Wall Street in the American Novel*. In this extract, Westbrook looks at the influence of Wall Street on the "social market."]

The role of the financial marketplace gains increasing visibility in Wharton's fiction after *The House of Mirth*. The relationships and dealings between people in society uptown become openly and directly explicable in terms of the commercial world downtown. For instance, the customs of Fifth Avenue take on the crass characteristics of Wall Street, not the country, in *The Custom of the Country* (1913). A New York society marriage is less an occasion of royal nuptials than a stock deal on a straight cash basis. Ralph Marvell, a scion of New York's Four Hundred, in the novel sums up the whole matrimonial situation: "The daughters of his own race sold themselves to the Invaders; the daughters of the Invaders bought their husbands as they bought on opera-box. It ought all to have been transacted on the Stock Exchange." Himself acquired like a blue chip equity, Marvell marries Undine Spragg, daughter of a newly rich Western millionaire.

The Spragg family from Apex city in *The Custom of the Country*, like Sim Rosedale in *The House of Mirth*, represents the invaders who began infiltrating New York in the 1880s. Undine, in her marriage transaction, picks up a social title in the manner of a robber baron raiding the stock of a nearly defunct railroad. In gaining control of Ralph Marvell, she proves an even more forcible and astute buyer than Rosedale, who tried but failed to swing a big investment deal for Lily Bart. The acquisition is short term, however, for Undine soon after her child's birth goes off to Europe and seeks a divorce. To understand this millionaire's daughter, "the answer would have been obtained by observing her father's business life. From the moment he set foot in Wall Street Mr. Spragg became another man." Undine's behavior in New York society, including her marriage, parallels her father's Wall Street speculative habits. Like him, she cares only for the quick-turnover profit, the short-term gain that comes from being on the "right side" of the market. Besides his investment objectives, Undine shares Spragg's determined Wall Street manner and code of ethics. Running off with Peter Van Degen, she thinks later that she acted "from a motive that seemed, at the time, as clear, as logical, as free from the distorting mists of sentimentality, as any of her father's financial enterprises." Her flight "had been as carefully calculated as the happiest Wall Street 'stroke.'" When she is back on the social market following her divorce, Undine assesses her own value as a purchasable commodity. She is motivated only by a desire "to get back an equivalent of the precise value she had lost in ceasing to be Ralph Marvell's wife. Her new visiting-card, bearing her Christian name in place of her husband's was like the coin of a debased currency testifying to her diminished trading capacity." Again, like her father, she makes an attempt in the market to recoup her losses. ⟨. . .⟩

—Wayne W. Westbrook, *Wall Street in the American Novel* (New York: New York UP, 1980): pp. 141–142.

CAROL WERSHOVEN ON RAYMOND DE CHELLES AND THE HYPOCRISY OF THE FRENCH NOBILITY

[Carol Wershoven is an associate professor of communications at Palm Beach Community College. She has published two books about Edith Wharton: *The Female Intruder in the Novels of Edith Wharton* and *Child Brides and Intruders*. In this excerpt from the former, Wershoven discusses Raymond de Chelles and the French nobility.]

Because the reader never sees Chelle's point of view, it is difficult to gauge exactly what, if anything, Raymond learns from his relationship with Undine. But the contrast of the American outsider and the French insider reveals not only the errors of American attitudes but the hypocrisies of French ways and their resemblances to certain American attitudes. Chief among the similarities of the two groups is the mercenary nature of their supposed romances. The marriage of Raymond and Undine is one of mutual exploitation, for Chelles expects to profit by it financially, as his brother Hubert does when he marries another American heiress, aptly named Miss Looty Arlington.

Whatever money is gained by these marriages, it is certainly not spent in enlivening the gloom of the family chateau, which supplies the boundaries of the narrow, suffocating world Undine has married into. If, as Elizabeth Ammons comments, Raymond is but a "nightmarish exaggeration" of Ralph Marvell, there is also a "nightmare quality," as Geoffrey Walton says, to the detailed descriptions of St. Desert, which is an even narrower and more repressive environment than Washington Square. And Chelle's genteel surveillance of Undine, with its veiled threats and quiet edicts, has its sinister side.

There is considerable hypocrisy in this restrictive world, for while Undine is carefully limited in her social life and acquaintances, others do as they please. Bored by Undine, Raymond seeks amusement elsewhere, enacting the scenario he had joked about at the Nouveau Luxe. And this is not just one more example of the double standard, for Raymond's cousin, the Princess Estradina, frequently shocks Undine with her tales of sentimental adventure. It is the Princess, with her frank, careless amorality, who represents a side of the Chelles family they would prefer to keep hidden.

There is not only a measure of hypocrisy in Chelle's actions, but a certain spurious quality to the man himself. The "lean, fatigued and finished" Count seems something of a *poseur,* for, just as Undine played the role of virtuous American during their courtship, so Raymond took the part of ardent suitor, and Undine seemed to sense that he was acting. Raymond's devotion to her before marriage "gave Undine the thrilling sense of breathing the very air of French fiction," and Undine does not easily lapse into fantasy without some stimulus. The sense of an innate phoniness continues. When the Chelles marriage is nearly over, Raymond delivers an empassioned tirade, accusing Undine of being like all other boorish Americans: "You come among us speaking our language and not knowing what we mean; wanting the things we want and not knowing why we want them; aping our weaknesses, exaggerating our follies, ignoring all we care about—", and this long and angry speech seems to come straight from Chelles's wounded, outraged core. However, the impact of it is somewhat distorted by the description of Chelles's face as he delivers it; he has "the look of an extremely distinguished actor in a fine part." Like Ralph Marvell, Raymond de Chelles likes to assume noble and superior attitudes, but in fact, he and his world are most vulnerable to the attacks of an intruder like Undine, who can imitate and exaggerate his weaknesses until they become apparent to all.

—Carol Wershoven, *The Female Intruder in the Novels of Edith Wharton* (London: Associated University Presses, 1982): pp. 68–69.

[Debra Ann MacComb is a Professor of English and Philosophy at the State University of West Georgia. She has published *Tales of Liberation, Strategies of Containment: Divorce and Representations of Womanhood in American Fiction, 1880–1920*. Here she discusses the commodification of divorce in *The Custom of the Country*.]

In characterizing divorce as "the home-made article", manufactured in America and superior to any French-Catholic annulment with which it might compete, Elmer Moffatt tacitly acknowledges its commodification as a product legalized, regulated, and sold by interests that profit from its consumption. A selling point to divorce seekers like Undine was a range of grounds capacious enough to fit almost any grievance. Like the cagey consumer she is, Undine explains to old Mr. Dagonet the product convenience such grounds afford the "disappointed" woman, enabling her to use any "trivial pretext": "Oh, that wouldn't be the reason *given*, of course. Any lawyer could fix it up for them. Don't they generally call it desertion?" Desertion is the reason she uses in suing Ralph for divorce, recognizing that its catch-all nature in some way sanitizes the proceedings. As Mr. Spragg tells Ralph, "[t]here wasn't any other plea she could think of. She presumed this would be the most agreeable to your family." Because divorces involving the social elite profit newspapers as well as lawyers, Undine takes advantage of the opportunity to retell and retail the story of her own disappointment "on the first page of [a] heavily headlined paper": "Society Leader Gets Decree . . . Says Husband Too Absorbed In Business To Make Home Happy." Recycled with variations that reduce the human and personal aspects of the breakup to the general, impersonal, and absurd, the story—cast as a typical modern day problem—finally makes its way to an advice column that promises its subscribers "a Gramophone, a Straight-front Corset, and a Vanity box among the prizes offered for its solution." Other businesses that spring up under the divorce umbrella include dressmakers who were beginning to provide outfits that were "not quite mourning, but something decently regretful" to observe the deaths of ex-spouses, and stationers who knew the correct form to use on a divorcée's visiting cards. ⟨. . .⟩

While divorce most certainly advances the interests of social climbers and profits those who capitalize upon its business opportunities, it also has its value for the old guard of New York society. As the "invaders" with their newly minted fortunes break down the barriers restricting entry into the exclusive circles, divorce becomes a marker used to distinguish—as money and leisure no longer can—the aristocracy from the upwardly mobile middle class. Although there "was no provision for such emergencies in the moral order of Washington Square," divorce within New York society nevertheless enables members of the old order to indulge in coded demonstrations of their superiority. The "black cashmere and two veils" that Ralph's mother dons to visit her "misguided" divorced friend is as much a costume of mourning as of concealment. Yet its double-veiled excess must certainly have been more conspicuous than concealing, drawing attention to her secretive "errand of mercy" and providing a display of social distinction that bespeaks largess even as it signifies removal from the "contaminated." Similarly, when Bowen (who has himself never married) holds forth on "the whole problem of American marriages" and "the key to our easy divorces," it is from a superior perspective. As he says, "I want to look down on them impartially from the heights of pure speculation"—heights defined by class as well as gender privilege. Thus distanced, Bowen can condescend to sympathize with "the poor deluded dears" who seek release from marriages "where all romantic values are reversed." Clare Van Degen can afford to adopt the attitude that divorce is "awfully vulgar" and Harriet Ray resolves "never to receive a divorced woman" because neither needs to enhance the value that her inherited name confers. Divorce thus determines a woman's worth and class: those like Undine who must use the courts to revalue themselves in the marriage market are like currency whose value is dictated by extrinsic forces; women like Clare are akin to real property whose value is based on intrinsic qualities and therefore less vulnerable to fluctuation. While divorce seems to promise upward mobility and social creditability, it proves the ultimate barrier to Undine's aspirations, barring her from "the one part she was really made for"—that of Ambassador's wife.

—Debra Ann MacComb, "New Wives for Old: Divorce and the Leisure-Class Marriage Market in Edith Wharton's *The Custom of the Country*," *American Literature* 68, no. 4 (December 1996): pp. 781–784.

Margaret B. McDowell on Choric Figures and Universalism

[Margaret B. McDowell is Professor Emeritus of Rhetoric at the University of Iowa at Iowa City. In addition to publishing *Edith Wharton,* she published a critical study of Carson McCullers. Here she discusses Wharton's use of minor, recurring characters to unify the story.]

⟨. . .⟩ Flashbacks may occur in any of the five books. For instance, Undine never returns to Apex, but Wharton sketches her life in Apex and Elmer Moffatt's background there through the recollections, which appear at various points in the novel, of Mr. and Mrs. Spragg, Undine, and Elmer. Frequent references to the Spragg's fashionably rustic summers in Skog Harbor and Lake Potash extend the canvas of the novel and introduce, with considerable economy, Undine's confidante and adviser, Madame de Trezak.

In addition to this retrospective technique, Wharton makes significant use of another technique of the dramatist—the choric figure who adumbrates, reflects upon, or interprets important events. Mme de Trezak is such a figure, but more important are Mrs. Heeny and Charles Bowen. Mrs. Heeny, a masseuse for society people, predicts Undine's future in the opening scene with her advice, "Go steady, Undine, and you'll get anywheres." Apparently classless, Mrs. Heeny claims to know "everybody" and looks impartially, but sympathetically, upon people in all classes. She cheers up Mrs. Spragg, explains to Undine the intricacies of invitations and of replies to them, carries in her bag clippings from the society columns that keep Undine informed about the activities of her peers and rivals, and provides Undine with cautionary advice about, or encouragement of, her enterprises.

Charles Bowen, an anthropologist, observes life with the detachment of a scientist and only occasionally generalizes about his reactions. At one point, for example, he concludes that most men become slaves to the marketplace in order to give money and social power to their wives; but the men feel too superior to the women to discuss their work with them. Ralph Marvell, he stresses, is an exception to the system; he prefers a leisured, genteel existence and a sharing of his inner life with his wife. Marvell is not likely, in Bowen's view, to survive in a shifting cultural scene in which qualities more vigorous than Marvell's will be at a premium. On the other hand, he regards Undine as "the monstrously perfect result of the system" that has tended to discount, in the worship of Mammon and the pursuit of power, the qualities of integrity and of consideration for others that Ralph symbolizes. It is Bowen who brings together two cultures, each motivated by a different kind of materialism, when he introduces Raymond de Chelles to Undine. In so doing, he is something like the scientist who confines two incompatible kinds of animals in a cage in order to watch their adaptations to their environment and to each other.

Some critics have regarded Undine's unscrupulousness as evidence that midwesterners had brought with them to New York the excessive materialism, the disregard for morality, and the deterioration of culture that Wharton thought dominated modern life. Such a critical view inadequately apprehends her satiric range; for she felt, to some extent, that the hypocritical Dagonets of this world were more vulnerable to close scrutiny than were the more open and forthright, though admittedly philistine, midwesterners. Similarly, Undine's frank acknowledgment of her financial needs and her direct approach to economic facts contrast favorably with Raymond de Chelles's pretenses, his unwillingness to recognize his poverty, and his resentment of the rich Americans with whom he associates.

Clare Van Degen's refusal to divorce her unfaithful husband and openly to acknowledge her love for Ralph Marvell springs from moral cowardice, from her conviction that divorce is "a vulgar and unnecessary way of taking the public into one's confidence." Mr. Spragg honestly states the principle that almost all the other characters live by: "I guess it's up to both parties to take care of their own skins." But only he recognizes that Undine must return the pearls she accepted from Van Degen. Plump and ridiculous, Mrs. Spragg appeals to one's sympathies because of her "stores of lymphatic patience." Princess Estradina's promiscuity shocks even Undine, despite her awe of royalty. The inescapable fact remains that Wharton satirizes dehumanizing materialism and rampant egotism in whatever social classes in America or abroad these attributes are dominant.

—Margaret B. McDowell, *Edith Wharton, Revised Edition* (Boston: Twayne Publishers, 1991): pp. 51–52.

[Claire Preston is the Graduate Tutor in Sidney Sussex College, Cambridge University. She has edited a collection of works by Sir Thomas Browne, and published a critical study of Wharton, *Edith Wharton's Social Register*. In this excerpt, Preston discusses Undine's placelessness as defining her "Americanness."]

Undine is an essential American literary figure: like Francis Parkman, Huckleberry Finn, and Dean Moriarty, American protagonists perpetually on their way to somewhere else, Undine can never 'arrive', just as she has no real place of origin or of rest, a quality signalled even in her bearing

> She was always doubling and twisting on herself, and every movement she made seemed to start at the nape of her neck, . . . and flow without a break through her whole slim length to the tips of her fingers and the points of her slender restless feet.

She is always tormented by the next thing, the better deal she may find in the next place, the 'peep through another door' giving 'glimpses of a more delicate kind of pleasure'.

Although Undine originates in the dismal boom-town of Apex City, and although she always invokes its social standards as an American benchmark, to say she is *from* anywhere in particular is too sentimental a reading of her origins, just as it is sentimental to imagine that her name has any traditional or intended spiritual significance. Apex is nowhere, or anywhere, its name as opportunistic as 'Undine'; it is an unmeant booster joke (like the real place in Illinois suggestively called 'Hometown'), a place being invented every day by shady boomers like Undine's father even as Undine reinvents herself. But Undine's placelessness is as necessary as it is typical: like the financier, she can only aggregate by ceaseless motion. Stasis is fatal to the stock-market, where fortunes are made from transaction on movement in either direction; so Undine is never at rest. Compelled by an obsessive, restless dissatisfaction with the status quo, at first she leads her weary parents around the nation in search of social standing and fashion until, in New York, she breaches the ramparts by marrying Ralph Marvell, and achieves, so she thinks momentarily, social apotheosis. Her whole existence has been devoted to the futile pursuit of fulfilment in an odyssey around ever-more-fashionable watering holes of the eastern United States, given over to the prodding ambition for the thing around the corner, in the next resort. Undine almost never goes back to the places she has been; she seems to use up each place she visits. She uses up a good half the American continent in her peregrinations before she marries Ralph Marvell in New York and briefly imagines that she has 'arrived'. By the end of the novel she has penetrated as far west as 'Dakota' and Nevada in search of divorce and remarriage, as well as the inner circles of New York and Parisian society. ⟨. . .⟩

Although Apex is imagined spatially, historically, and socially, mainly through Moffatt's doings, it is nevertheless a place which yields only the placeless. Those who seem to come from Apex never stay there because they do not belong there or anywhere. Two other characters from the novel follow Undine out of Apex—Indiana Frusk, the plumber's daughter, now Indiana Frusk Binch Rolliver; and Moffatt himself, even more rootless than Undine, who appeared one day in Apex, whose origins are unknown, and whose meteoric career allows him to keep surfacing in every part of the globe. Moffatt's history, as we have seen, is a narrative lurking beneath the surface of the Undine story, and his first 'steal' is Undine herself. This is a piece of inside information which would rock the New York social world as much as the Ararat investigation disrupts the financial world. But nomadism provides protective camouflage: Old New York, like Wharton herself, isn't very clear about the geography of 'the West', and no New Yorker can know of Undine's peccadilloes there. It also transpires that Undine was even earlier engaged to Millard Binch, son of a local Apex merchant; that she jilted him for Moffatt; and that once jilted, he married Indiana Frusk, who by the time she enters the story *in propria persona* has divorced him in order to marry Congressman James J. Rolliver. Rolliver, in turn, is betrayed by Moffatt, who testifies about irregular land deals in Apex, but later becomes his partner against Driscoll. In Wharton's notes for the original ending of the novel, Undine marries Rolliver after divorcing Moffatt. If Undine's absurd name confounds any normative standard of belonging—being as fortuitous as the hereditary, traditional names of the Old New York and Old Parisian families are deliberate, as whimsical as the current chase after the latest thing— the insouciant marital and romantic bonds of the Apex characters seem to create their own interbred, intermarried clique, a social tribe, a vigorous, midwestern parody of the labyrinthine cousinages and interfamilial alliances of Old New York.

—Claire Preston, *Edith Wharton's Social Register* (New York: St. Martin's Press, Inc., 2000): pp. 119–121.

Plot Summary of
The Age of Innocence

The Age of Innocence opens in a typically Whartonian setting: the opera. The juxtaposition of the introduction of the main characters of the novel with the description of operatic show suggests that perhaps the "real" people in the novel may not be so different from the opera's actors. This theme of costume and recitation (as opposed to naturalness and spontaneous communication) informs Wharton's descriptions of the New York society in which she sets her novel.

The story is told primarily from the perspective of Newland Archer, a member of the respected "old" New York society. He sees his fiancée, May Welland, across the opera house in her family's box; she is accompanied by her cousin, Ellen Olenska. Ellen was raised in Europe by her unorthodox aunt Medora Manson, and married the Polish Count Olenski. Rumor has it that she recently abandoned her (probably abusive) husband and ran away with his secretary. Concerned that Ellen's reputation (and her family's seeming willingness to forgive it) might damage May, Archer suggests that he and May announce their engagement that night; he would then be considered "family" and Ellen would have *two* influential families supporting her (the Wellands and the Archers). May understands and appreciates Archer's purpose: "Nothing about [Archer's] betrothed pleased him more than her resolute determination to carry to its utmost that ritual of ignoring the "unpleasant" in which they had both been brought up."

Mrs. and Mrs. Lovell Mingott plan a dinner in order to welcome Ellen back to New York; in silent protest against Ellen's actions, all but two of the invitees refuse to come. At the request of Archer's mother, Henry and Louisa van der Luyden (cousins of Mrs. Archer) agree to intervene. As the most respected members of "old" society, the van der Luydens' support of Ellen guarantees her a place in society. They plan a dinner themselves and invite Ellen as a guest of honor; as expected, those who had previously refused to meet Ellen now welcome her.

Archer calls on Ellen the day after the dinner, and that evening sends May a bouquet of lilies-of-the-valley, and sends Ellen yellow roses, which "did not look like [May]—there was something too rich, too strong, in their fiery beauty." For Archer, the two women represent antinomies of femininity. May represents "old" society decorum, purity, and innocence (represented by white lilies), while Ellen stands for naturalness, sensuality, and honesty (yellow roses). His interactions with Ellen make him uneasy and dissatisfied with his role in society; thoughts of May serve to calm him and restore his faith in tradition.

Archer works at a law firm; because he is "family," he is given the case concerning Ellen's divorce. He convinces Ellen to drop her suit on account of the embarrassment it would cause her family, but is strangely disappointed at her easy acquiescence to an argument based on social propriety.

May and her family visit St. Augustine, and Archer goes to the opera alone. Again he sees Ellen, and the two converse flirtatiously. The following day, Archer feels anxious about his marriage. He feels as though his life is split between "Tradition" and "Reality," or, as he comes to see it, between May and Ellen. He understands that he enjoys "Tradition" because he is able to counter it with "Reality": good conversation, artists, his journalist friend Ned Winsett. But Archer wonders, "once he was married, what would become of this narrow margin of life in which his real experiences were lived?" He writes to Ellen, discovers she is visiting the van der Luydens at their estate in the Hudson Valley, and follows her. They meet in the restored Patroon house and confess that they have romantic feelings for one another. The arrival of Julius Beaufort, with whom Ellen may be having an affair, halts their conversation. Archer is upset by Beaufort's intimacy with Ellen, and returns to New York.

Three days later, Ellen, back in New York, writes Archer and asks him to visit her. He panics, and in order to stifle his thoughts of Ellen, flees to St. Augustine to see May. He begs her to push forward the date of their wedding, and May asks him if he loves another woman. Archer denies this, both to May and to himself. By marrying May as soon as possible, Archer will no longer be tormented by his conflicting feelings concerning femininity and society; he imagines that his marriage to May will make the decision for him, on the side of Tradition. May refuses, and Archer returns to New York.

Archer calls on Ellen, and her aunt Medora privately tells him that Count Olenski is attempting to convince Ellen to return to him. Medora asks Archer to advise Ellen to reconcile with her husband. Ellen and Archer speak privately and confess their love for one another; Archer asks Ellen to marry him. She refuses, reminding him that she is still married because he advised her not to sue for divorce. They are interrupted by the arrival of a telegram from May, thanking Ellen for helping to convince Mr. and Mrs. Welland to move forward the wedding date. Archer leaves immediately.

Book II opens one month later at Archer and May's wedding. Medora comes to the service, but Ellen is absent; Archer has not seen her since the night he proposed to her. We next see Archer and May in London, at the end of their three-month wedding journey. At a dinner party, Archer meets Monsieur Rivière, a French tutor and scholar; they have an interesting conversation, and Archer suggests to May that they invite him to dinner. May refuses, saying that he was "dreadfully common." Confirming his fears, his marriage prohibits him from indulging in conversation with "non-members" of his social set.

The story skips forward, and it has now been one-and-a-half years since Archer has seen Ellen. His set is in Newport for the summer, and one day he sneaks away from May in order to find Ellen. He discovers that she just left for Boston, and follows her, excusing himself "on business." Ellen went to Boston to meet an "emissary" from her husband, who is still trying to reconcile. She refuses to return to him. Archer and Ellen spend the day together as a couple. She promises she will not return to her husband as long as she does not become a temptation for Archer; she refuses to have an affair with him.

On the train back to New York, Archer sees M. Rivière; he was the "emissary" from Count Olenski. Archer suspects that he is also the secretary who helped Ellen flee from her husband. M. Rivière confesses that he thinks Ellen should stay in New York, and begs Archer to help keep her there. He tells Archer that all of Ellen's family thinks she should return to her husband; they have been excluding Archer from all discussions on the subject.

Four months later, Ellen has not returned to her husband; her family is upset, and she moves to Washington. Her grandmother,

Mrs. Mingott, cuts off her allowance, so Ellen's money depends on Beaufort's generosity. Archer longs to see her, and finally tells May that he must go to Washington on business. May asks him to visit Ellen; May seems to be aware of Archer and Ellen's true relationship. Before Archer can visit Washington, however, Beaufort, due to shady business deals, is ruined financially. His wife is a distant relative of Mrs. Mingott and begs her for help; the scandal of Mrs. Beaufort attempting to abandon her husband causes Mrs. Mingott to have a mild stroke. At the request of her recovering grandmother, Ellen comes to New York.

Archer meets Ellen at the train station. In the brougham on the way to Mrs. Mingott's, they kiss, then argue because Archer refuses to accept their current separation. Ellen insists they maintain a distance between them, arguing that "We're near each other only if we stay far away from each other. Then we can be ourselves. Otherwise we're only Newland Archer, the husband of Ellen Olenska's cousin, and Ellen Olenska, the cousin of Newland Archer's wife, trying to be happy behind the backs of the people who trust them." Archer gets out of the brougham and walks home alone.

The next day, Mrs. Mingott tells Archer that Ellen has decided to stay with her in New York indefinitely. Archer sees Ellen's decision to stay as her compromise; rather than leaving New York (and tempting Archer to follow her), she will stay and become his mistress. They both, however, find the situation distasteful, and Ellen says that she may return to her husband after all.

The next evening, Archer attempts to confess to May his feelings for Ellen, and ask her to set him free. As soon as he says Ellen's name, May interrupts him to say that Ellen is returning to Europe, but not to her husband; May insists on throwing her a farewell dinner. The dinner occurs ten days later, and Archer realizes that everyone (including May) thinks he and Ellen are having an affair, and that all are happy she is leaving because they have finally succeeded in separating the pair. Archer plans to abandon May and follow Ellen to Europe; after the dinner, he tells May that he would like to go away on a long trip alone. She tells him that is impossible because she has just learned that she is pregnant.

The final chapter serves as an epilogue; the setting is twenty-six years later. Archer and May remained together and had three children. Archer worked briefly in politics, and is considered "a good citizen." May died two years before of pneumonia. Their eldest son, Dallas, is engaged to Fanny Beaufort, the illegitimate daughter of Beaufort and Fanny Ring. Dallas convinces Archer to join him on a trip to Paris. In Paris, Dallas looks up Ellen and surprises Archer by taking him to her home. But Archer refuses to go up to her apartment; he sits on a bench outside, thinking, "It's more real to me here than if I went up." Eventually, a servant comes out onto Ellen's balcony and lowers the shutters; Archer sees this as a silent communication, and returns to the hotel. ✽

List of Characters in
The Age of Innocence

Newland Archer is the central character in the novel. The plot centers around his engagement and marriage to May Welland, and his love for May's controversial cousin, Ellen Olenska.

May Welland is a representative member of "old" New York society; she marries Newland Archer. She is Ellen's cousin, and Mrs. Mingott's granddaughter.

Countess Ellen Olenska is May's cousin. She was raised in Europe by her aunt Medora Manson. She married and separated from her abusive husband, a Polish Count, and returns to her family in New York. Archer falls in love with her, but is already engaged to May.

Julius Beaufort, is a "foreign" banker who has settled into New York society. He has an affair with Ellen, and with a woman named Fanny Ring. His illegal business transactions lead to his financial ruin.

Mrs. Julius Beaufort (**Regina**) is married to Beaufort. After her husband's financial ruin, she pleads for help from her great aunt, Mrs. Mingott.

Mrs. Manson Mingott is the grandmother of May Welland and Ellen Olenska. She is eccentric but tolerated because of her wealth and social standing.

Mr. and Mrs. Henry van der Luyden are the pillars of "old" New York society. They live on their estate in the Hudson Valley, and come into the city only for special occasions. Mrs. van der Luyden (Louisa) is a cousin of Archer's mother, and at Mrs. Archer's request, they come into the city to show their support for Ellen when she first arrives.

Mrs. Medora Manson is Ellen's aunt, and Regina Beaufort's cousin. She raised Ellen after her parents died. She has had several husbands, and "old" New York society does not wholly approve of her, or of her liberal upbringing of Ellen.

Ned Winsett is a member of New York's group of "artists"; he knows Archer. He provides a contrast to the decorum of New York society. Ellen befriends him and his group when she arrives in New York.

Monsieur Rivière was Count Olenski's secretary, and helped Ellen leave him. There are rumors that he and Ellen had an affair. Archer meets him in London, then again in Boston when M. Rivière attempts, on the behalf of Count Olenksi, to persuade Ellen to return to her husband.

Mr. Sillerton Jackson is an older member of "old" New York. He is known as the authority on "Family," and knows the history and gossip about all of his peers.

Lawrence Lefferts is an acquaintance of Archers; although he is married, he is known for his womanizing. He is the authority on "Form" in "old" New York society.

Dallas Archer, Archer and May's first son, takes his father to Paris at the end of the novel. He is engaged to Fanny Beaufort, the illegitimate daughter of Julius Beaufort and Fanny Ring.

Mrs. Lemuel Struthers is mentioned throughout the novel, but never appears. She is representative of "new" New York society: she ignores many of the rules of decorum (e.g., she entertains on Sundays). At the beginning of the novel, she is uniformly shunned by Archer's group, but by the end, she has become tolerated.

Mrs. Thorley Rushworth is a married woman with whom Archer had an affair before the start of the novel. ❁

Critical Views on
The Age of Innocence

GARY H. LINDBERG ON NEW YORK'S "SCREEN OF CUSTOM"

[Gary H. Lindberg (1941–86) was a Professor of English at the University of New Hampshire, which established the annual Lindberg Award in 1986. He published *The Confidence Man in American Literature* and *Edith Wharton and the Novel of Manners*. Here he discusses the way New York society functions as an exclusive group, and the way custom dictates its response to invaders.]

We are confronted with a society that concentrates on the foreground of experience, that is alive to particular manners as evidence, not of acceptance or exclusion, but of propriety or disintegration. The informing quality of old New York is the complex system of interpretation accompanying its manners, and the subtle, discriminating cast of mind shared by old New Yorkers indicates both the strength and the weakness of this system. The refined interpretation of behavior is based on an acute sense of "good form." Throughout the novel particular observations are filtered through a screen of custom; we are constantly reminded of the way things have always been done. Archer arrives at the ball late, "as became a young man of his position," and we learn in a characteristic parenthesis that the "young bloods" usually go to the club after the opera. The rigidity of these customs suggests a rough equivalence in the various ways of "going too far"—there seems to be no way of distinguishing the bad form of a young man coming on time to a ball and that of the Mingotts bringing a "disgraced" countess. The system thus encourages disproportionate responses—Archer cannot simply defend the Countess Olenska, he must "champion" her. His phrasing of his determination during the ball to "see the thing through" reveals a standardized response in which lapses from good manners appear in moral formulas.

The weaknesses of this system are most evident when the New Yorker encounters new ways of behaving, as Archer does when he first visits Ellen Olenska's house in the "Bohemian" quarter. By having Ellen herself out when Archer arrives, Wharton contrives a scene in which the young man can respond to the setting while he waits; she then illustrates the effects of that setting on his personal relationship with Ellen. The curious thing about Archer's view of her room is that he cannot see much. He spots a few details—some slender tables, a Greek bronze, a stretch of red damask—and his mind darts away. Most of the particularities of interior decoration in his mind do not involve Ellen's house at all but a projection of the house in East Thirty-ninth Street where he and May will live. He cannot come to terms with the unforeseen style of Ellen Olenska except by referring back to the interiors he has learned to see. As in the description of the Beaufort ball, the analysis here sets the scene historically and emphasizes signs of change. Young architects are striking out from the uniformity of New York's brownstone, and the freer spirits who have read Charles Eastlake's *Hints on Household Taste* (first published in America in 1872) have learned how to rebel against the ornamental excrescences of the Victorian interior. Thus Archer assumes that May will simply carry on her parents' style— "purple satin and yellow tuftings . . . sham Buhl tables and gilt vitrines"—whereas he will break away from the conventional by arranging his library as he pleases, "which would be, of course, with 'sincere' Eastlake furniture, and the plain new bookcases without glass doors." His smug sense of originality blinds him to the fact that the lines of his rebellion have already been laid down. The conventions themselves are changing, and, like New Yorkers attending Beaufort's ball, Archer is simply moving with the times.

But how does his mental excursion into New York's interior decorating help him place Ellen's house? Her style does not fit, and Archer's perceptions are so bound up in the conventional that he cannot see her drawing room specifically. Instead he feels "the sense of adventure"; he confronts the scene abstractly ("the way the chairs and tables were grouped") and stylizes its effect—"something intimate, 'foreign,' subtly suggestive of old romantic scenes and sentiments." The New Yorker's intense concentration on the surface of life makes him acute in recognizing deviations from the customary— "only two Jacqueminot roses (of which nobody ever bought less than a dozen)," "perfume that was not what one put on handkerchiefs"—but such scrutiny also places undue emphasis on the mere fact of deviation. The unusual becomes the "foreign," and because of New York's blending of manners and morals, the foreign is associated with the suggestive and the romantic. Instead of assessing the arrangement of a room, Archer finds himself confronting something alien, immoral, and extraordinarily enticing.

—Gary H. Lindberg, *Edith Wharton and the Novel of Manners* (Charlottesville: UP Virginia, 1975): pp. 102–3.

CYNTHIA GRIFFIN WOLFF ON ARCHER'S CHOICE

[Cynthia Griffin Wolff is the Class of 1922 Professor of Literature at the Massachusetts Institute of Technology. In addition to editing the Norton edition of *Ethan Frome,* she published *A Feast of Words: The Triumph of Edith Wharton, and Emily Dickinson.* Here she examines the effect on Archer of Ellen's arrival.]

Though Ellen's arrival has had the objective effect of hastening Newland's public commitment to May, it has at the same time made that commitment seem a sentence to death by asphyxiation. When Newland retreats to his study to sort out the various effects of Ellen's appearance, he finds that her case has "stirred up old settled convictions and set them drifting dangerously through his mind." His image of Ellen balances conveniently and simplistically against an image of May as "the young girl who knew nothing and expected everything"; and the larger vistas of the twilight world from which Ellen has come diminish the appeal of a marriage that seems no more than "a dull association of material and social interests held together by ignorance on the one side and hypocrisy on the other." Central to these images of the women in Archer's life is some picture of what he is to become himself. This scene in his study is but the first in a series of increasingly terrifying invocations of self; the future stretches before him, "and passing down its endless emptiness he saw the dwindling figure of a man to whom nothing was ever to happen." In fearing acceptance into the "hieroglyphic world" of old New York, Archer really fears anonymity and personal insignificance.

Yet he is hindered more by his own habits of thought than by insufficiencies in the society around him, for his impatience with specific details and intractable actualities follows him in his quest for personal identity. Just as it is easier to deal with the "case" of Ellen than with Ellen herself, so it is easier to pursue an image of personal fulfillment that is uncomplicated by the details of everyday living. Throughout much of the novel Archer longs for a life that moves well beyond the charted realms of the familiar, a life of high emotional intensity and sustained moral and intellectual complexity. The kind of life he only hazily conjectures is a life that is, given the "harsh world" of human experience, available to only a very few; and Archer seems an unlikely candidate for the life that his imagination yearns toward.

Ironically, the danger that his life will be insignificant lies not so much in the probability that he will fail to fulfill these fantasies as in the more immediate possibility that, having failed to fulfill them, he will lack the capacity to give *any* aspect of his life authenticity. Not all things are possible for a man of Newland's time and place; some ways of life that are unavailable to him are, perhaps, better than any that are. But every real life involves compromises and relinquished hopes—even though some lives require more in the way of sacrifice than others. The problem that Newland faces without fully comprehending it is that his desire to create an ideal self substantially hinders him from infusing some *genuinely possible* self with meaning.

To be specific, if the passion that Ellen has finally released in him is eventually thwarted by his failure to effect a relationship with her, then he might not manage to attach these emotions to any part of the life he actually leads. Like Ralph Marvell, he might drift back into idle, empty dreaming. He might never attain the capacity for sustaining deep and meaningful bonds with others. He might become a hollow man altogether. This danger is the central problem that he faces.

And in this respect, Newland's quandary captures the quintessential problem of all who grew to maturity in the repressive society of old New York. Perhaps he will settle for a set of highly stereotyped personal relationships that serve only to mask a deep sense of isolation and incompleteness. Perhaps he will even go through his entire life never feeling that he is really "himself"—even though everyone else seems to think that he is "somebody." It is a horrifying specter.

—Cynthia Griffin Wolff, *A Feast of Words: The Triumph of Edith Wharton* (New York: Oxford UP, 1977): pp. 317–139.

Margaret B. McDowell on Archer's Limited View: May vs. Ellen

[Margaret B. McDowell is Professor Emeritus of Rhetoric at the University of Iowa at Iowa City. In addition to publishing *Edith Wharton,* she published a critical study of Carson McCullers. Here she discusses the ways in which Archer's prejudices color his perception of May and Ellen.]

Wharton reveals Archer's limited views, subtly and ironically, at the very times that he is complacently evaluating, from the heights of his presumed sophistication, the limited views of others, particularly those of May. Charmed by Ellen Olenska's imagination and experience, he nevertheless reacts with hypocritical conservatism when he refuses to acknowledge her need to divorce a cruel and unfaithful husband. To openly recognize her bitter experience would be to acknowledge that a woman of his wife's family understands from wordly experience too much about sex. Archer's temptation to be unfaithful to May ultimately helps him achieve a greater honesty about himself; he is now able to recognize that passion and moral convention are sometimes strongly at odds. As a result of his admitting his own passions and his ultimate desire for an illicit affair with Ellen, he attains a degree of tolerance for those outside his own circle of complacent and morally "superior" aristocrats.

Regarding his relatives and friends as the whole world early in the book, he assumes that Ellen's naïveté prevents her from being impressed by the party that the Van der Luydens give for her. In Archer's circle, everyone recognizes that this party is the Van der Luydens' gesture of acceptance of Ellen—an acceptance reluctantly accorded by other aristocrats because she has returned to New York without her husband. As a matter of fact, Ellen's worldly knowledge makes her refuse to attach to the party the radical significance that Archer and his friends see in it. Ellen wants only to be accepted for what she is, not forgiven for something that is not her fault. Because Newland's friends still believe in the import of such social gestures, the farewell party that May gives for Ellen also assumes importance because for them it symbolizes the end of Newland's presumed affair with Ellen.

If he initially misjudges Ellen for her supposed inability to react according to his expectations at the time of the Van der Luydens' party, he also misjudges May by viewing her as more limited than she is. Before their marriage, he simply assumes that she will never be capable of surprising him with "a new idea, a weakness, a cruelty, or an emotion." Ironically, he is himself incapable at this time of recognizing her resentment of his affair with Mrs. Rushworth or her courage in suggesting that he marry his former mistress. He does not recognize the stratagems to which May resorts in order to keep him from leaving with Ellen, nor does he realize her lasting gratitude to him for giving up Ellen. His egocentric temperament, which limits his imagination, prevents him from seeing May as a woman instead of a stereotype. He fails to see that what he calls "her abysmal purity" is a myth largely of his own formulation—one that underestimates her intelligence, the extent of her worldly knowledge, her strength, and her capacity to fight for her interests.

Though May appears to Archer and her male contemporaries as an image of ethereal purity and as a helpless being, she is in Wharton's evaluation a woman of considerable strength. For one thing, May enjoys sports—at that time largely reserved for men. Twice Wharton refers to May's big, athletic hands—when May displays her ring and later when she tries dutifully to sit by her husband and do delicate needlework with hands meant for rowing and archery. May's interest in extending their honeymoon to Italy lies largely in the additional opportunities there to walk, ride, swim, and play tennis. Her skilled performance in "a feat of strength" at the Newport archery contest adds dimensions of competence and assurance to her character and aligns her, both in her apparently chaste temperament and in her prowess, with Diana. She also develops much resourcefulness when Ellen threatens to undermine her hold on Archer—a toughness and a tenacity of purpose that show she is more than the clinging, helpless woman so much cherished as the New York aristocrats' ideal.

—Margaret B. McDowell, *Edith Wharton, Revised Edition* (Boston: Twayne Publishers, 1991): pp. 62–64.

[Marilyn R. Chandler is Wert Professor of American Literature at Mills College and the author of *A Healing Art:
Regeneration Through Autobiography* (Garland, 1990). Here
she examines Wharton's use of symbolic architecture, particularly in private homes.]

Wharton teaches us in this novel to read architecture and interior
decoration, and indeed the entire environment of fabricated
objects, as an intricate network of symbolic systems that make vis-
ible and reinforce the behavioral mores and severe social stratifica-
tion whose implications are so consistent an issue in her work.
Living space is always significant space, never free of moral reso-
nance from the moment the colors are chosen for the curtains.

Houses provide an index not only of social position but of individual psychology. The stately old mansions inhabited by
Wharton's little clan of patrician New Yorkers—the Mingotts, the
Archers, the van der Luydens, the Beauforts—are not only mea-
sures of their wealth and taste but also, in a more subtle fashion, of
their priorities, their authority, their recognition of consensually
decreed standards of taste and behavior, and their various degrees
of hesitancy to depart from these standards. The acute aesthetic
sensitivity of the narrator's often ironic descriptions of furniture,
fabrics, and facades reminds us that every house and every object
within it reflect a choice, if only a choice to conform to prevailing
fashion, and that these choices have moral and psychological as
well as aesthetic consequences. The relationship of character to
environment is emphatically reciprocal, and the houses the characters inhabit influence them as surely as these houses reflect the
characters' influence.

Mrs. Manson Mingott's house, the first to be fully depicted, is
described in terms of its idiosyncratic departures from architectural and social proprieties. It is "cream-colored" rather than the
more conservative and more fashionable brown. It sits in lonely
splendor, as defiantly distinctive as the spirited old matriarch who
sits "enthroned" within it, "waiting calmly for life and fashion to
flow northward to her solitary doors." She seems oddly oblivious to
the binding imperatives of tribal conformity and behaves "as if

there were nothing peculiar in living above Thirty-fourth Street, or in having French windows that opened like doors instead of sashes that pushed up." Hers is an earned impunity. Her eccentricities are tolerated by dint of long service to convention and an unquestioned seniority as matriarch of a large and devoted clan and are excused as well because she belongs to the tightly knit inner circle only by marriage: her mother was a Spicer of Staten Island, not one of the first families of Manhattan.

Newland, through whose eyes we see and judge this architectural oddity, interprets its eccentricities of style with a skilled and critical, yet admiring, eye, only too aware of the stringencies of the codes Mrs. Manson Mingott has so blatantly defied:

> A visit to Mrs. Manson Mingott was always an amusing episode to the young man. The house in itself was already an historic document, though not, of course, as venerable an certain other old family houses in University Place and lower Fifth Avenue. Those were of the purest 1830, with a grim harmony of cabbage-rose-garlanded carpets, rosewood consoles, round-arched fireplaces with black marble mantels, and immense glazed bookcases of mahogany; whereas old Mrs. Mingott, who had built her house later, had bodily cast out the massive furniture of her prime, and mingled with the Mingott heirlooms the frivolous upholstery of the Second Empire.

The ironic phrase *grim harmony* suggests Newland's own discomfort with prevailing taste but is offset by the condemnation of Mrs. Manson Mingott's Second Empire furniture as "frivolous." His observations are as detailed as his tastes are decided at this early stage in the story; if he is capable of regarding the old woman's oddities with indulgence, he is equally capable of issuing judgments as opinionated as those of Lawrence Lefferts, the "foremost authority on 'form' in New York," until Newland's complacencies are shaken by the aesthetic and moral awakening he experiences when he enters Ellen Olenska's home and life.

—Marilyn R. Chandler, *Dwelling in the Text: Houses in American Fiction* (Berkeley: University of California Press, 1991): pp. 157–158.

[Carol Wershoven is an associate professor of communications at Palm Beach Community College. She has published two books about Edith Wharton: *The Female Intruder* and *Child Brides and Intruders.* In this excerpt from the latter, Wershoven discusses the threat that Ellen poses to New York society.]

Ellen disturbs others not only because of what she dismisses, but because of what she values. She cares about ideas; she even has books in her drawing room, "a part of the house in which books were usually supposed to be 'out of place.'" And she mingles with writers and artists, those people who terrify the rich New Yorkers.

And, worst of all, Ellen takes New York's slogans seriously. When she is cautioned that any happiness "bought by disloyalty and cruelty and indifference" is a despicable happiness, she believes it. And, believing, Ellen acts on her faith. Her greatest social error is to accept, as a standard of behavior, the values her group has long since abandoned. She accepts society's pretense as reality, thus holding the insiders to their own words. That they are hypocrites is repeatedly made clear by their attempts to buy their own happiness with acts of disloyalty and cruelty and indifference to Ellen herself. ⟨...⟩

Ellen is posing a double menace to New York: she threatens because she doesn't value what New York really worships (money), and because she does value the loyalty, generosity, and discipline New Yorkers only pretend to live by. As long as Ellen remains in New York, she continues to be dangerous. Her very presence, even as a married woman, challenges the sanctities of family and class. And it challenges the complacency of Newland Archer as well.

At the same time that Ellen upholds the value of family solidarity, she subverts the stereotypes that support it. The New Yorkers live by the easy categorizations that permit them never to think; one such categorization defines the wife in a broken marriage as the guilty partner. Ellen's decision to leave the count automatically relegates her to this role, but her demeanor and behavior do not fit it. While the insiders are eager to condemn Ellen and gossip incessantly about her friendship with the notorious Julius Beaufort, they cannot be sure that Ellen has become a "bad" woman. Appearances suggest that she may simply enjoy male friendship. She is surrounded by men who admire her: the writer Ned Winsett, the Duke of St. Astrey, the patriarch Mr. van der Luyden, the financier Beaufort, the count's secretary, Monsieur Rivière. The idea that a woman can relate to men on a basis that is neither sexual nor filial is a new one in New York.

And the list of Ellen's friends is troubling for another reason. The mix of aristocrat and servant, of artist and businessman indicates Ellen's blithe disregard of the class lines that mean so much to the ruling families. Ellen calls the duke "dull," mocks the van der Luydens' exclusivity, mixes with the *arriviste* Mrs. Struthers, lives among artists and writers, and visits academics. Ellen is interested in ideas, not social identity, and if the Shoe-Polish Queen, Mrs. Struthers, can offer her good music, Ellen will seek her company. She creates her own fashions, but in doing so, she weakens the barriers that have protected and even created old New York's power. The insiders, like their leader, old Mr. van der Luyden, have achieved influence through exclusivity. But Ellen is blurring the lines of insider and outsider, dismantling a sacred structure.

Whenever Ellen troubles the insiders, they send an emissary from their world to negotiate with her. But Newland Archer cannot restore Ellen to the world of innocence; instead, she lures him farther and farther outside. She reverses his values; she makes him see. With Ellen, Archer learns to look within the Valley of Childish Things and beyond it. He credits her with "opening my eyes to things I'd looked at so long I'd ceased to see them," and once he recognizes the deadliness of the child-world, he begins to dream of a different one. Archer is learning to move beyond his world in dreams, yet he can never do so in reality.

—Carol Wershoven, *Child Brides and Intruders* (Bowling Green: Bowling Green State University Popular Press, 1993): pp. 228–230.

[Pamela Knights is a Lecturer on American literature at
the University of Durham in England. In addition to
Wharton, she has published articles on William Faulkner,
and edited the Oxford edition of *The Awakening: And
Other Stories*. Here she discusses the extent to which *The
Age of Innocence* is a story about money, focusing on the
trajectory of Julius Beaufort.]

If unregulated women trouble New York, so does unregulated capital. Perhaps because the novel makes its points so succinctly, some
readers have felt that *The Age of Innocence* is less interested in the
dynamics of money than is some of Wharton's earlier fiction. But
from start to finish, the text has money on its mind: its sources,
legitimacy, and limits. Whereas it distributes different aspects of
femininity between a set of different characters, it largely concentrates finance into one: that of Julius Beaufort. Like Ellen, he is a per-
petual riddle in the narrative: any answers only produce the same
question: "Who was Beaufort?" We meet him as a New Yorker by
custom, but at every appearance in the text he sets up currents of
disquiet. Like Simon Rosedale in *The House of Mirth*, he is an outsider, possibly Jewish (he "passed for an Englishman"), whose
rumored excesses set whispers murmuring "not only in Fifth Avenue
but in Wall Street." Whether in monetary or sexual versions, Beaufort is viewed in terms of spending, with all its suggestion of fluidity,
bleeding, giving out too much, being used up: "Some people said he
had speculated unfortunately in railways, others that he was being
bled by one of the most insatiable members of her profession; and to
every report of threatened insolvency Beaufort replied by a fresh
extravagance."

Lavish outgoings, speculation, risky investments, tainted capital,
all run counter to the image of the self as constituted in leisure-class
New York. Good form restrains other men. (Lefferts's mistresses do
not drive bright-yellow carriages at the fashionable hour.) Cautious,
conservative, resistant to indiscreet expenditure, New York reins in
passions and capital; the self remains solvent, its moral and its business consciences sound, and its identity clear. While Beaufort simu-
lates integrity, he is acceptable. Once he over-reaches, his smash

threatens the whole of New York: "'Everybody we know will be hit one way or another.'" As both sexual and financial disasters rise to a crisis, shock waves pass through society. Mr. Letterblair, the family's legal conscience, is left "white and incapacitated," and in the body blow to "Family," Mrs. Mingott suffers a stroke. Less "mysterious" to readers than to her relations, Beaufort's fall registers the worst that can happen—an intolerable rupture at the center of New York that lays it open shamefully to the world: "That afternoon the announcement of the Beaufort failure was in all the papers. . . . The whole of New York was darkened by the tale of Beaufort's dishonour."

> —Millicent Bell, ed., *The Cambridge Companion to Edith Wharton* (Cambridge: Cambridge UP, 1995): pp. 33–34.

KATHY A. FEDORKO ON ELLEN'S INDIVIDUALITY

[Kathy A. Fedorko teaches at Middlesex County College. She has published *Gender and the Gothic in the Fiction of Edith Wharton,* from which this excerpt is taken. Here she examines Ellen's inability to assimilate into New York society.]

In a first edition copy of *The Age of Innocence* presented to Katherine Cornell, who played Ellen in the 1928 stage rendition of the novel, Wharton wrote, "With admiration and gratitude to Katherine Cornell, whose art has given new life to the wistful ghost of Ellen Olenska. EW July 1929." Wharton's reference to Ellen as a ghost supports the character's own comments about herself as having died and returned to a spirit life. When Newland mentions that she has been away a long time, Ellen answers "Oh, centuries and centuries; so long . . . that I'm sure I'm dead and buried, and this dear old place is heaven" (ellipsis mine). Later, before they are reunited, Newland remembers Ellen as simply "the most plaintive and poignant of a line of ghosts." When she subsequently tries to explain her inner journey confronting the Gorgon to Newland, her explanation "seemed to come from depths of experience beyond his reach." As she acknowledges, "You've never been beyond. And *I* have. . . . And I know what it looks like there" (ellipsis mine).

It is just such an internal strength that strikes Newland about Ellen, a quality both mysterious and enthralling. There is about her, not youthful prettiness, but "the mysterious authority of beauty, a sureness in the carriage of the head, the movement of the eyes, which, without being in the least theatrical, struck him as highly trained and full of a conscious power." She looks at him with "eyes so deep," "meditative eyes," and possesses, he feels, the "mysterious faculty of suggesting tragic and moving possibilities outside the daily run of experience," possibilities he yearns to know but can't.

Ellen's "passionate honesty" and "conscious power," the by-products of having faced her fundamental being, allow her, while she is back in New York society, to stay receptive to values not her own while remaining strong against the absorbing pull of collective standards. Having experienced nothingness, she is also able to be alone, in fact relishes it. As she explains to Newland, part of "the blessedness" of her "funny house" is being alone in it as long as her friends keep her from feeling lonely. The mature self-acceptance implied by this feeling, that one enjoys oneself *and* the company of others, is echoed by Wharton's own comments to Mary Berenson after Berenson's nervous breakdown. The "only cure," Wharton wrote her, is "to make one's centre of life inside of one's self, not selfishly or excludingly, but with a kind of unassailable serenity—to decorate one's inner house so richly that one is content there, glad to welcome any one who wants to come and stay, but happy all the same in the hours when one is inevitably alone."

Ellen's story in *The Age of Innocence* is of her realization that she *cannot* cast off the mature self she has become, cannot "wipe out all the past" and live in blissful oblivion as she initially thinks she wants to. Unlike the motherless Lily Bart in *The House of Mirth*, who never loses her longing for oblivion, the motherless Ellen is supported in her transitional period of neediness by two surrogate mothers, her Aunt Medora and her grandmother Catherine. Their attentiveness and affection enable her to reclaim her mature role as "pour-soi," a changing, self-defining individual, and to avoid seeking self-worth and power through a man. The two older women provide her with a strong female heritage, for they are models of untraditional, even eccentric womanhood. They encourage self-reliance and intriguing individuality in Ellen rather than the restrained "factitious purity" typical of Old New York women. And as in the best mothering,

Medora and Catherine allow Ellen to outgrow them, to surpass them in self-knowledge and initiative. Until Ellen reaches this point they provide the financial and emotional support that allows her to nurture herself. In terms of the Gothic text as Wharton is developing it, the two women are living, humorous amalgams of mythical mothers, Medusa and the "Great Mother."

—Kathy A. Fedorko, *Gender and the Gothic in the Fiction of Edith Wharton* (Tuscaloosa: University of Alabama Press, 1995): pp. 89–91.

Works by
Edith Wharton

"Mrs. Manstey's View." 1890.

The Decoration of Houses (with Ogden Codman). 1897.

The Greater Inclination. 1899.

The Touchstone. 1900.

Crucial Instances. 1901.

The Valley of Decision. 1902.

Sanctuary. 1903.

The Descent of Man. 1904.

The House of Mirth. 1905.

The Fruit of the Tree. 1907.

A Motor-Flight Through France. 1908.

Artemis to Actaeon. 1909.

Ethan Frome. 1911.

The Reef. 1912.

The Custom of the Country. 1913.

Fighting France. 1915.

The Book of the Homeless (Editor). 1916.

Xingu and Other Stories. 1916.

Summer. 1917.

The Marne. 1918.

French Ways and Their Meanings. 1919.

The Age of Innocence. 1920.

In Morocco. 1920.

The Glimpses of the Moon. 1922.

A Son at the Front. 1923.

Old New York. 1924.

The Mother's Recompense. 1925.

The Writing of Fiction. 1925.

Twilight Sleep. 1927.

The Children. 1928.

Hudson River Bracketed. 1929.

Certain People. 1930.

The Gods Arrive. 1932.

A Backward Glance. 1934.

Works about
Edith Wharton

Ammons, Elizabeth. "The Business of Marriage in Edith Wharton's *The Custom of the Country.*" *Criticism* 16 (1974): 326–38.

Auchincloss, Louis. *Edith Wharton: A Woman in Her Time.* New York: Viking, 1971.

Barnett, Louise K. *Authority and Speech: Language, Society, and Self in the American Novel.* Athens: University of Georgia Press, 1995.

Bendixen, Alfred and Annette Zilversmit, eds. *Edith Wharton: New Critical Essays.* New York: Garland, 1992.

Benstock, Shari. *No Gifts from Chance: A Biography of Edith Wharton.* New York: Scribners, 1994.

Bjorkman, Edwin A. "The Greater Edith Wharton." *Voices of Tomorrow: Critical Studies of the New Spirit in Literature.* New York: Mitchell Kennerley, 1913.

Bloom, Harold. *Edith Wharton.* New York: Chelsea House, 1986.

Coxe, Louis O. "What Edith Wharton Saw in Innocence." *New Republic* 27 (June 1955): 16–18.

Deegan, Dorothy Y. *The Stereotype of the Single Woman in American Novels.* New York: Octagon, 1951.

Donovan, Josephine. *After the Fall: The Demeter–Persephone Myth in Wharton, Cather and Glasgow.* University Park: Pennsylvania State University Press, 1989.

Doyle, Charles C. "Emblems of Innocence: Imagery Patterns in Wharton's *The Age of Innocence.*" *Xavier University Studies* 10 (1971): 19–25.

Edel, Leon. "Summers in an Age of Innocence: In France with Edith Wharton." *New York Times Book Review,* June 9, 1991.

Erlich, Gloria. *The Sexual Education of Edith Wharton.* Berkeley: University of California Press, 1992.

Fetterley, Judith. "'The Temptation to Be a Beautiful Object': Double Standard and Double Bind in *The House of Mirth.*" *Studies in American Fiction* 5 (1977): 199–211.

Fryer, Judith. *Felicitous Space: The Imaginative Structures of Edith Wharton and Willa Cather*. Durham: University of North Carolina Press, 1986.

Gimbel, Wendy. *Orphancy and Survival*. Landmark Dissertations in Women's Studies. Edited by Annette Baxter. New York: Praeger, 1984.

Goodman, Susan. *Edith Wharton's Women: Friends and Rivals*. Hanover and London: University Press of New England, 1990.

Hays, Peter S. "Wharton's Splintered Realism." *Edith Wharton Newsletter* 2.1 (Spring 1985): 6.

Howe, Irving. *Edith Wharton: A Collection of Critical Essays*. Englewood Cliffs, New Jersey: Prentice–Hall, 1962.

Joslin, Katherine. *Women Writers: Edith Wharton*. London: Macmillan, 1991.

Kaplan, Amy. "Edith Wharton's Profession of Authorship." *ELH* 53.2 (Summer 1986): 433–57.

Kazin, Alfred. "Afterword." *Ethan Frome*. New York: Collier, 1987.

Lawson, Richard H. *Edith Wharton*. New York: Ungar, 1977.

Lewis, R. W. B. *Edith Wharton: A Biography*. New York: Harper and Rowe, 1975.

Lewis, R. W. B. and Nancy Lewis, eds. *The Letters of Edith Wharton*. New York: Charles Scribner's Sons, 1988.

Lyde, Marilyn Jones. *Edith Wharton: Convention and Morality in the Work of a Novelist*. Norman: University of Oklahoma Press, 1959.

Murad, Orlene. "Edith Wharton and *Ethan Frome*." *Modern Language Studies* 13 (Summer 1983): 90–103.

Nevius, Blake. *Edith Wharton*. Berkeley: University of California Press, 1953.

Niall, Brenda. "Prufrock in Brownstone: Edith Wharton's *The Age of Innocence*." *Southern Review: An Australian Journal of Literary Studies* 4 (1971): 203–14.

Orr, Elaine Neil. *Subject to Negotiation: Reading Feminist Criticism and American Women's Fictions*. Charlottesville: UP of Virginia, 1997.

Ransom, John Crowe. "Characters and Character: A Note on Fiction." *American Review* 6 (January 1936): 271–88.

Rose, Alan Henry. "Such Depths of Sad Initiation: Edith Wharton and New England." *New England Quarterly* 50 (1977): 423–39.

Rusch, Frederick S. "Reality and the Puritan Mind: Jonathan Edwards and Ethan Frome." *Journal of Evolutionary Psychology* 4.3–4 (1983): 238–47.

Showalter, Elaine. "The Death of the Lady (Novelist): Wharton's *House of Mirth.*" *Representations* 9 (1985): 133–49.

Tuttleton, James, and Kristin O. Lauer and Margaret P. Murray. *Edith Wharton: The Contemporary Reviews.* New York: Cambridge, 1992.

Vita-Finzi, Penelope. *Edith Wharton and the Art of Fiction.* New York: St. Martin's, 1990.

Walton, Geoffrey. *Edith Wharton: A Critical Interpretation.* Rutherford: Farleigh Dickinson UP, 1970.

Wolff, Cynthia Griffin. "Lily Bart and the Beautiful Death." *American Literature* 46 (1974): 16–40.

Index of
Themes and Ideas